PRAISE FOR *WITHIN*

"Martin Nowak, an eminent mathematician and scientist, takes us on a voyage of exploration, not only through this universe of changing things, but into the realm of eternal realities that underlies it—the realm of mathematical truth, of unchanging laws that govern change, of the essences and forms the intellect grasps, of the love that draws the soul toward beauty and goodness, of the Logos that is within all things and upholds all things. It is a quest that goes 'within': into the human soul, 'that place where the temporal and atemporal meet,' where God awaits you as a teacher; into the inmost self; into the heart that can be wounded and inflamed by the fire of God's love. Guiding us on this quest are great philosophers, theologians, sages, and saints, among them: Plato, Aristotle, Augustine, Aquinas, the great Carmelite mystics, and St. Thérèse of Lisieux. Part dialogue, part reverie, part dream, this unique book is an intellectual and spiritual ascent that opens endless vistas that will leave the reader forever changed."

—**STEPHEN M. BARR**, President of the Society of Catholic Scientists, Professor Emeritus of Theoretical Particle Physics, University of Delaware

"In his book *Within*, Martin Nowak presents a masterpiece of intellectual and spiritual synthesis, interweaving timeless philosophical insights with profound truths of faith. He crafts a Cathedral of thought inviting readers to traverse the infinite corridors of reason and revelation. Evoking Borges's *Library of Babel*, this work challenges and inspires us to contemplate life's greatest mysteries by unveiling a divine order that resonates with both faith and reason. In his artful blending of mathematics, theology, and philosophy into a symphony of love and truth, Nowak's *Within* becomes not merely a book to be read, but a journey to be lived—a testament to the grandeur of creation and the inexhaustible depths of divine mystery. Here is treasure for all who seek wisdom and the ultimate meaning of existence."

—**SANTIAGO SCHNELL**, William K. Warren Foundation Dean of the College of Science, Professor of Biological Sciences, Professor of Applied & Computational Mathematics & Statistics, University of Notre Dame

"Seldom is scientific brilliance coupled with poetic virtuosity, but Martin Nowak is that rare combination. His *Within* should help convince a new generation that empirical knowledge and religious faith are not at odds, any more than are truth, goodness, and beauty. Indeed, his text plausibly suggests that neither body nor soul, neither time nor eternity, is intelligible without God. No library and no librarian should be without *Within*; its epic multiverse is a 'confluence of wisdom and kindness.'"
—**TIMOTHY P. JACKSON**, Bishop Mack B. and Rose Stokes Professor of Theological Ethics Emeritus, Candler School of Theology, Emory University

"*Within* entrancingly follows Martin Nowak's earlier tone-poem, *Beyond*, in escorting the reader to a realm of Platonic idealism and Christian sanctity where mathematics, science, philosophy, and theology converge in a unique vision of divine and human love. Along the way much is learned about classical metaphysics, but the encounter with the great Carmelites John of the Cross and Thérèse of Lisieux represents the unforgettable climax of the drama. Here is a book to transform our consciousness, both philosophically and spiritually."
—**SARAH COAKLEY**, FBA, Norris-Hulse Professor of Divinity Emerita, University of Cambridge

"*Within* unfolds a rare world of thought and belief. Through an extended dialogue, it weaves together evolution and mathematics, science and Platonic Forms, naturalism and God. The result is like nothing I have ever read before."
—**MARTIN PUCHNER**, Byron and Anita Wien Professor of Drama and of English and Comparative Literature, Harvard University

"*Within* is a remarkable synthesis of science, philosophy, theology, poetry, drama, and suspense, offering a compelling account of how mathematics and biology lead to God, fused with spiritual meditations on Divine Love that are astonishingly beautiful and profoundly moving."
—**ANDREW LOKE**, Associate Professor of Religion and Philosophy, Hong Kong Baptist University

"*Within* is a beautiful contemplation of the evolution of the soul toward God—the guiding teacher within, who is infinite Love. It is philosophy and prayer, as well as poetry. It is catholic in its reach into diverse areas of knowledge and in its vision of the scope of God's providential work. It inspires the very love that is its subject."

—JOSEPH LAPORTE, Professor of Philosophy, Hope College

"In its explorations of fundamental questions about God and the universe, Martin Nowak's latest book *Within* is like a modern version of Lucretius's *De Rerum Natura*. His elegant style blends narrative suspense with poetic metaphor, taking readers on a journey of profound scientific discovery and deep religious contemplation."

—MIRELA OLIVA, Professor of Philosophy, University of St. Thomas, Houston

"Building on his contemplative novel, *Beyond*, Martin Nowak now offers us a mystical poem, *Within*. The journey within, we learn, is inseparable from the journey outward: mathematics, physics, evolution, philosophy, and theology are integrally woven into the mystical ascent. Relationships and love grace this narrative of devotion, indispensable steps on the way to the Source of Love. Reminiscent of Teresa of Ávila's *Interior Castle* and Thérèse of Lisieux's *Story of a Soul*, this is not just a book to be read, but a path to be walked."

—PHILIP CLAYTON, Ingraham Professor, Claremont School of Theology

WITHIN

WITHIN

BY MARTIN NOWAK

Angelico Press

CONTENTS

how powerless i am to express in words the secrets of heaven
— St. Thérèse of Lisieux

arise! awake! walk with her
through the empyrean library
with its endless corridors
grand rooms and open doors

enter the cathedral of infinity
marvel at the dome of books
behold pillars carrying heaven

explore the lush gardens
where Forms are thriving
under cedars of Lebanon

ascend the mountain of Love
visit the elysian monastery
view the ocean of Truth

hear words which will never pass
read the books written for You
find the path that leads Within

MOVEMENT
I

years after her death scholars found access
to the limitless library she had described
they were amazed by the vast geometry
offering a transfinity of books and shelves

some concluded the library represented
an unbounded universe resting in itself
the number of books was estimated to be
of the cardinality called countably infinite

there were not more and not fewer books
than prime numbers under the triple stars
those prime numbers as everyone knew
were created by God emerging from truth
while all else was a human invention

the scholars assumed that the library had
the ability to answer questions about her
the library represented a quest for purpose
a generative grammar to trace her path
an algorithm for finding the laws of nature

while many aspects were carefully revealed
novel questions arose as the centuries passed
the nature of the library came under scrutiny
pointed battles arose amongst eager academics

scholars who devoted their erudite energies
to study the library joined competing camps

first were those who affirmed the library existed
and did so independently of any human activity
next came those who accepted the library existed
but needed to be derived from bits and atoms

third were those who held the library was only
a mental construct of deep neuronal networks
finally arrived those who said that the library
did not exist at all but was only a name

each learned faction had convincing reasons
to defend their stance, none embraced plurality

one day a novice named John of St Matthias
found deep inside the transparent castle
a room resembling the office of a librarian

on a desk in that room rested an open book
as if someone had been reading it moments ago
but wherever he looked no one was to be seen
however long he waited no person returned

as the book was open his gaze fell on words
not in want of time he began to read within

she had been wandering through the library
with an ever-increasing all-consuming curiosity

first she had surmised she was in Borges's library
but now she questioned that initial assumption
for whenever she opened a book and read within
she found meaning and words that spoke to her

how unlikely that was if the library contained
all sequences of letters in combinatorial space

while in Borges's library it was not impossible
to find books which conveyed some message
it was still exceedingly improbable to do so

but then life was not uniformly distributed
over those unbounded probability measures
her voluntary actions may not be random
her choice of books could be gently guided

some principle could make her select books
that made sense but which law of nature
or of mathematics would certify to that?
what chooses among attainable realizations?

here were the options she contemplated:
if the library contained all possible books
and yet she found meaning in her path
which well-disposed spirit guided her hand?

if the library contained only certain books
and still there were infinitely many of them
which net had sieved that vast collection?

wandering through a world of meaning
and being part of it evokes those questions
what is the device that creates meaning?
which mechanism guides your trajectory?

what is the relationship between books and life
between life and dreams? how is the library linked
to the unfolding path of an expanding universe?
which demiurgic principle joins words to events
forms to instantiations, possibilities to actualizations?

is the library recollecting what happens outside
or is the world performing what is written within?
does the library anticipate a future or recall a past?
in what direction are the arrows of causality aimed,
the slingshots accelerated by semi-rational lenses?

it became more evident that she needed to find
a librarian who could answer some of her questions
she began to envisage him as a resourceful teacher
who provided guidance in the realm of possibilities

❊ ❊ ❊

after the experience of many pages and books
crossing light years of passage she found him
the librarian!—or rather as she thought: a librarian
because the tamed multiverse of shelves certainly
demanded fastidious crowds of hard-working keepers

the librarian appeared to her as if purposefully
stepping out of a narrative to be of service

she was pleasantly surprised by the chance encounter
which she attributed to her unmerited good fortune
she resolved to ask him for structure and guidance

perhaps he could convey how to see the library
in a way that would be meaningful to her and
later—as a consequence—beneficial to all people

maybe it was God's choice that her poor life
had an effect on the world however minute

as she approached the librarian was writing
but seeing the peculiar way that his hand
moved over the paper made her conjecture
he was not blessed with the sense of vision

a blind librarian amidst an infinity of books!
was this an opportunity to be of service?
the librarian was dressed in a hooded robe
he was a monk belonging to a pious order

good father, she began her polite address
forgive me for interrupting your precious work
i have stumbled upon this room perchance

pausing she noted how sound dominated
color and light in the room of the librarian
words were illuminations coming from within
at once he stopped his activity of writing

while i had hoped to find a wise librarian
who could teach me it is no design of mine
to be of any nuisance or impose on anyone
rather than distracting your valuable activity
i wonder if i could be of service to you

seeking only truth in my striving i humbly ask:
what does the library mean? how am i to use it?
... how are we to use it? she corrected herself
since she was inserted here to speak for all souls

his head moved up, his face turned to her
who stood at the sill of the door of his cell
which he had kept open for all those years

seeing his eyes she saw he did not see hers

although her steps had been noiseless
her words had been perceived by him
as well as the hope arising from them

my Lady, he said, you are here at last!
you have arrived! ... be most welcome!

speaking was not easy and demanded effort
he needed to clear his throat more than once
his voice had not been used for a long time

did you expect me, good father? she wondered

i knew you would come, my Lady, but not when

for sure you are most welcome! he repeated
the expression on his face was one of absolute joy
intermixed with the fragility of advanced age
the confluence of wisdom and kindness moved her

may i ask how you knew i would come? she said

it is written in the books, he answered

is it written that someone would come
or written that i would come? she inquired

that is the same, he replied

the answer surprised her—as we can imagine
yet she deemed it impolite to press the matter

can i be of help to you, good father? she asked

certainly, my Lady, certainly! he answered
the harvest is plenty and the workers are few
lady seemed more fitting than *demoiselle*
which he had encountered in reference to her

likewise i am overjoyed to offer my services to you
behold i am the librarian! he announced with dignity

it is an impressive library! she congratulated him

i have every reason to be fond of it, he admitted

did you help to assemble the vast collection?

oh no! he laughed, you overestimate my abilities
he was amused by that particular consideration

do you help maintain the library? she asked

it does not need much maintenance, he replied

do you add new books? she wondered

new books are being added continuously
but this is not my doing, it just happens

are you ordering the books? she asked

i have been thinking about this problem
but i admit i have never solved it, he said

solved what? she wondered

whether an efficient algorithm for ordering exists

forgive me, good father, but then may i ask
what is the task of a librarian in this place?

my purpose is helping you find what you seek
a librarian is a diligent guide, a teacher, a friend
for the search is long and the goal is uncertain
the moment is fleeting and experience is slippery

i see that this is a noble charge, she exclaimed
i welcome a teacher in this mesmerizing place
a friend is a blessing sent by the merciful God
i am glad i found you, i am looking forward
to assisting you in return in any way that i can
but know, good father, my abilities are limited

modesty is a virtue, he answered with a smile

it is not modesty that speaks but simple truth
she replied, for i know that i know nothing

yes, yes! he said, i have read that line before
he moved his head in search of certain books

may i ask: how can i help you, good father?

let us start our journey with reading, he proposed
reading in a library is the activity of the blessed
reading is akin to walking through this world
with the resolve to learn, with the hope to find

then after some reading you may choose to write
thereby helping the books to become living matter
once the books are alive evolution can act on them
they become deeds along the trajectory of the soul
thus it would give me joy if you were to read to me

i am very happy to oblige, where shall we begin?
she looked around, which book may i read to you?

any book will do, he replied

any book? she asked

any book! he affirmed

that is, a random one?

if you like ... a random one

do you want me to choose a book in this room?

either in this room or in any other, he answered

she walked along the great wall of books

the book chooses the reader, he murmured

excuse me? she said turning toward him
welcoming the opportunity to delay her choice

the Queen does not resemble her portrait
instead the portrait resembles the Queen
he substantiated his enigmatic remark
albeit with meager success for now

she shrugged her shoulders and made a choice
she placed the book carefully on the table
then she opened it and began reading within

in this pellucid voice you deign to reveal
precious secrets to your servant, he thought

slowly awakening he was trying to find himself
vaguely he recalled tranquility and drifting in space
had she read a book to him while he fell asleep?
had they been in a book they were reading together?
was there word of an infinite limitless library?
or had she visited the realm of the death
and obtained from there the secret of life?

then it dawned on him: they had been in a library
they were in a book and the book was in the library
it was the library of Babel that contained every book
every sequence of letters combinatorically possible
with punctuation and space inserted for convenience
orwithneitheronenortheotherasinthoseancienttimes
tosavespaceonpreciousmarbleorsumptuousgranite

but in Borges's library all books had the same length
while in theirs the number of pages per book varied
some of the books were brief while others were long
testing the commitment of the most devoted reader

Borges's famed library was likened to a genome space
where all sequences had the same number of bases
in their library, however, genomes differed in length
thereby resembling a biology which waxes and wanes
does evolution unfold within unchanging spaces?
does evolution explore possibilities that are given?

he could not remember now—slowly awakening
if they had concluded there must be an upper length
to a book that was privileged to inhabit their library
he knew no empirical way to resolve that question
he thought half-awake, unless the library was finite

physically there should be a maximum to the length
of a material book...but what if only some books
were printed while others resided in capacious clouds
not clouds obstructing suns, not clouds making suns,
but genuine mathematical ones coeternal with truth

even if he had slept among semi-instantiated books
physics did not govern proceedings within their library

their own experience revealed that the library was static
without the smallest evidence of gravitational collapse
if those ominous books had mass the library would dwarf
an imposing gaggle of multiverses feeding on dark energy

questions about the library—he remembered now—
are of mathematical nature rather than of physical law
perhaps the library was part of some overarching reality
a kind of Platonic heaven populated by propositions

the library did not reside in the spatiotemporal world
but objects in the library could be in specific locations
certainly you can ask where does a particular narrative
occur in a normal number for the first of many times

he now recalled the theme that had amused his sleep:
being a dedicated realist he could rest in that library
while anti-realists needed to dispute its real existence
which—for consistency—should keep them awake
if they got stuck within it however tried and tired

those anti-realists were renowned trouble makers
although they were useful at keeping the field fertile
controversy after all was the cherished breadwinner
of fearless philosophy not in want of waste bins
it fueled learned seminars, renewed grant applications
and provided pleasant gatherings in esoteric locations

you needed highly trained, well-spoken opponents
for principled stage fighting with pen and paper
to hammer away at a keyboard is to be at war!

he loved games even if they had no useful equilibria
in game theory opponents are called co-players
this convention turns anti-realists into co-players

the concept of an anti-realist was a Platonic Form
existing in underlying reality without any need
to be derived from instantiated or other matter

if all deniers of real forms were suddenly to disappear
—he was unsure if that was a delightful fantasy or not—
the real form of a denier would still be left behind
and this form would not even stand in the dark
because it would readily be illuminated by Her
since in Her infinite wisdom she shines on all forms
even those attempting to deny and undo her

counterfactually—if all realists were removed
from the instantiated realm then the anti-realists
would think they had won the competition and
the form of the good would leave them in peace

amusingly if anti-realists wanted to be consistent
they had to maintain there was no such thing as
an anti-realist but if there was one—hypothetically
—then it would have to be a Platonic Form

moreover they would never agree to capitalize
Idea or Form which realists did occasionally
was any decency left in the void post modernity?
was there any respect for ontological commitment?

the discipline that consisted of elaborate footnotes
to if not the first but surely the greatest philosopher
of the occident had reached by unguided evolution
a lamentable demise or a rebellious life in the shadows
depending on worldview—did he dream all of this?
what else was in his dream? oh yes! how congenial!

she was reading to him while he had fallen asleep
and then he dreamt about her in sumptuous decor

there was a sunset in autumn with opulent trees on fire
they were rushing to a concert with Gustav and Ludwig
who projected shadows making further growth of music
in the classical domain difficult if not entirely impossible

the first had intended to edit the second's ninth
with the honest ambition of improving the oeuvre
translated and improved was the enticing footnote
of Shakespeare's first translation into Yiddish

even magnificent forms—such as the ninth—
were not entirely protected against the pen
of well-intended colleagues who composed
the problem was in the fourth movement

what happened prior? what happened before
they were walking downhill in the sunset?

had she been running through a summer rain?
was her hair covered with myriads of raindrops?
was each droplet a glittering pearl of elementary waves
solving Schrödinger's equation for open universes?
was each wave traversing a field of complex numbers
while each normal number pronounced all books?

she shook those libraries from her hair and then
—to his considerable surprise in untamed dreams—
she wore no libraries ... anymore ... anywhere
at once he was fully awake!

❀ ❀ ❀

sweet dreams? she asked

he saw her at a distance sitting at a desk
engaged in the calm activity of writing
she was wearing a white morning robe
while her hair was loose and down

the space around her shone in elegant simplicity
the furniture of the room was in the style of the last
but one Queen in the line that was never to break

the walls of the room were covered with books
they were aligned in shelves from floor to ceiling
the light that pervaded the room came from her
and from the windows that were wide open

yes thank you, he answered, good morning

he looked at her with great devotion
as if she was the sole uncaused cause
of all goodness that existed in the world

briefly looking up she smiled for him
then she continued her composition
being focused seemed effortless for her

talent hits a target no one else can hit
genius hits a target no one else can see
he thought not seeing what she was writing

forgive me for asking, what is the purpose
of writing in a library that contains all books?

does the library contain all books? she asked
or does it offer only infinitely many?

infinity is a large number, he answered

some infinities are smaller than others, she said
and we are called to participate in the creation

are you writing this book? he wondered

what makes you think so? she asked

how else could i find meaning, he replied

you are an open book to me, she answered

if we are in a book are we in a library? he asked

books have a tendency to be in libraries, she said

is there coffee? he wondered changing the subject

over there you will find, she responded

over there was accompanied by a motion of her eyes
after which they re-engaged the page of production

seeing the coffee made his senses come alive
this library is a wonderful place! he thought

if coffee were not yet counted among Platonic Forms
then somebody should think about putting it there
waking up in Platonic heaven required coffee
it belonged to the public domain of available goods!
he continued meandering in his morning philosophy

may i ask about the purpose of the book
which you are writing? he inquired

all activity in the world has one purpose:
to empower souls to fall in love with God

to this end i wish to sing the praises of the Lord
for it is honorable to publish the work of God
but i am simply holding a pen gliding over paper
while the book of nature and the science of love
dictate the content of what ought to be written

i am only a brush in the hand of the artist
i do not want to interfere with His design
for only the Celestial Painter could compose
the images i wish to convey in the story of my soul

will you read the book to me one day?
he inquired while pouring coffee into two cups

we will read it as we go along, she replied

will we explore the library together? he asked

we will walk through the library, she confirmed
but i need you to be patient, my rested realist
because even in the expanse of an infinite time
we can only see a vanishingly small fraction of it

being able to sleep in a limitless library
is one thing but walking through it is another
if you dream about books they come to you
if you long to read books you must go to them

there is also the garden which we should see

a garden? he asked curiously

the one of the Forms, she replied

a garden of the Forms . . . how amazing!
does it contain all Forms? he wondered

she left the question unanswered

meanwhile the morning light grew stronger
together with the fragrances and noises
that entered through the open windows
it made him feel that life was new

walking through the library they saw magnificent rooms
that would at opportune times attract admiring visitors
but also inconspicuous ones whose fate it was to be ignored
she preferred the quiet rooms as they contained hidden acts
which had no great name on earth but were loved by God

do not strive to be the most beautiful tree in the world
she told him one afternoon in an iridescent sunlit parlor
but rejoice if there is a blossom on one of your branches
exult if a word of love coming from you finds a heart

when they opened a book in one of the reticent rooms
their eyes encountered the words: *Does God exist?*

do not be surprised to find the question in this library
it is part of God's eternal plan for His creation, she said
in the city of the world this question is ubiquitous

can you enlighten this citizen? he wondered

the question would not exist in the realm of human hearts
if God had not lovingly placed it there for our growth
therefore God has granted the question to occur within

the existence of the question is the sign of a gentle love
God works relentlessly without forcing Himself on us
God wants to be found and the question leads to Him

in the temporal realm, the question *Does God exist?*
can emerge from worries, from limited perspectives
we wonder: what if the material realm is all there is?
what if there is nothing that awaits us after death?
even saints have been troubled by such questions

all souls need to experience some uncertainty
for growth in love toward God, she continued

temptations against hope are nourishment for the soul
weakness enables us to help others in similar states
frailty binds us together, failures prepare us for eternity
a teacher needs to grasp what her students are missing
a Queen ought to experience what her people endure

she was silent as they walked on

the rooms of the library grew successively larger
in all places were books which followed on books
was the library a mandala? an image of the cosmos?
were entire libraries within books, he wondered
was the space unbounded? who has measured it?

the search for God is central to every human soul
she continued, the question *Does God exist?*
is asked by many people in one guise or another
at some point in their lives either openly or in secret

the question remains with us as we move through life
the question sharpens our tools of ontological inquiry

the question is formulated to prepare the way
to discover the world, to illuminate domains
to probe for purpose, to find meaning in life

life poses and answers the question anew every day
the question is present when we aim to understand
the realm in which we live, the existence we have

it is the first question of all systems yearning for truth
the search starts with the question and returns to it
the question is a crucial one that grounds philosophy

excluding the question suspends us over a fragile foundation
the question is a human attribute—we have always asked it
we are the being that ponders the question with fervor
homo sapiens is a religious creature drawn to spirituality

they were now strolling through a part of the library
that appeared medieval, many books were manuscripts
tall windows—painted or clear—provided illumination

the two types of glass indicate two ways to God, she said

faith and reason? he conjectured

theology and philosophy, she answered

theology proper and philosophical theology? he asked

the middle ages saw a separation of the two, she replied
sadly in my opinion as you can imagine

Does God exist? accompanies the temporal trajectory
since the essence of God which is the existence of God
cannot be comprehended by anything outside of God

thus the question lingers on and is painful for some
the freedom to love comes with the freedom to doubt

if the question were not present the three virtues
faith, hope, love would not be the gifts they are
without uncertainty love would not be what it is

could you please explain this to me? he asked

one saint loves God from a point of certainty
she sees God face to face and experiences unity
with Him in unbreakable and tender embrace
the other saint loves God from a place of doubt
from a dark prison without spiritual consolation

which is the greater love?

probably the second, he replied

if a saint wants to be Love what would she long for?

both, he answered looking at her now

some souls linger in uncertainty and doubt
but Love wants to be present to all souls
therefore she wants to sit on the same table
with those who experience no consolation

are you talking of a particular saint?

be patient! her glance seemed to suggest
for your encounter has not yet occurred

the corridor they had been traversing opened
to a larger structure that looked like a plaza
in the midst of it was the fountain of time passing
next to it stood an obelisk that served as a witness
on the far side of the plaza arose a cathedral

Shimon bar Yonah was a jew from Judea
a peregrinus, an apostle of Jesus from whom
he received the keys to the kingdom of heaven

from their perspective he could not yet discern
if the cathedral was built of ancient stone or of books
in any case it was so large that it seemed unbounded

this part of the library, the cathedral, she explained
is dedicated to the question: *What is God?*

is it as unbounded as it appears to be? he asked

Does God exist? constitutes a finite subset, she said
What is God? is an infinite subset of the library
the first question will come to an end eventually
but the second question remains with us in eternity

why is this? he asked

it takes forever to get to know an infinite being, she said

loving someone gives you a glimpse of that experience
if you truly love someone she will remain inexplicable
each moment you wonder: who is she? what is she?
what are her thoughts? why am i blessed to know her?

What is God? includes what is the meaning of God?
how is God revealed to us? what can we know about God?

how is God present in all, in the material universe
in the laws of nature, in the realm of mathematics
in the lives of people, in the witness of saints
in the teachings of wisdom, in sacred scripture?

have prophets spoken to us? what was their message?
what can we learn about God at moments in spacetime?
are holy signs pointing to God wherever we strive
reaching from a world of change to an unchanging one?

they had now entered the celebrated cathedral of infinity

Does God exist? What is God? induce three more questions:
What exists? What can be known? What is our purpose?

ontology, epistemology, ethics! he exclaimed with fervor
the celebrated pillars that hold the building of philosophy

not more, not less! she affirmed with one of her smiles
she granted him despite the grandeur that surrounded them

then the question really induces all of philosophy, he thought

the library holds philosophy and theology together, she noted

they reached the three columns which carried the structure
looking up at them he noted that the ceiling was out of sight
whatever they held was distant, beyond the reach of mortals

the cathedral of infinity, she said, when God built his own churches
everything here consists of books, that is of the Eternal Word
the columns, the floor, the benches, the apse, the choir, the crypt
the altar and the windows that admit the Light of the World!
as you can see the Spirit proceeds from the Father and the Son

filioque, he remarked, but where can i see this?

philosophy is an edifice rooted in heaven with concepts
coming down to us, she replied, gazing up at the columns

but questions about God are not satisfied by words
the answers must include the entire life you lead
the union of your actions, the totality of your love
the sacrifices you offer, the people you support

the answer has to do with finding yourself
that is your innermost self and letting go of it
to receive it anew from God in each moment
be an empty vessel ready to accept God's love!

do you follow me? she asked

wherever you strive! he replied

i want you to succeed, she said

if you love God you let go of yourself to receive
the gift of your existence anew every moment

faith is our response to God, she continued

Gaudium et spes, he remarked

you are full of surprises, she laughed

i have read something, he said apologetically
as you have asked me to do: *tolle lege!*

it is of benefit to consult the wisdom of the written word

when they first had entered the immense cathedral of infinity
they had lowered their voices of respect for the house of God
and not to disturb others who were there but they saw no one

why is this church empty? he wondered

be patient! it will not remain empty, she answered

faith is our response to God, she continued
the response must come from personal conviction
from searching for truth, from opening our heart
the response must be based on reason and on love
which work together to establish ultimate concern

ultimate concern? he asked

proper religious attitude induces ultimate concern
its object is experienced as overwhelmingly real
in comparison profane attractions are mere shadows

a gesture of her hand made those shadows disappear

the object of ultimate concern is a maximal being
or a fearless quest for the good but often it is both

a search for the Form? he wondered—she nodded

how would you describe maximal being? he asked

we are at the place where i want us to be, she said

do you mean the two of us in particular? he wondered

all people ought to be lovers of wisdom, she replied

Does God exist? has led us to the question *What is God?*
and from there onward to *What is a maximal being?*
here all rational objections to God's existence come to naught

why is this? he asked

you must define maximal being in a limited way
in order to be able not to believe in Her existence
this particular approach is called local atheism
it proposes a limited concept of God which is rejected
but a limited concept is not a maximal being
the theist can readily agree with the atheist
in rejecting a version of god which is implausible
local atheism helps to clarify what God is not

global atheism however means the rejection
of any concept of God that can be proposed
global atheism is logically indefensible:
you cannot reject the existence of God
for all possible meanings of the term

not even nihilism gets you there in one piece:
for if you answer the question *What exists?*
with *nothing* then also atheism does not exist

What exists? is an entertaining question, he offered
someone argued *everything* is a possible answer

the answer is amusing but i do not embrace it, she replied
rather my conjecture is that the category of everything
that exists is not definable by a finite collection of rules

why do you adopt this perspective? he asked

for mathematical and theological reasons, she said

both of those made him now think of Gödel
whose incomplete bust was about to be unveiled
in the courtyard of the university they had visited

because God who causes existence cannot be measured
either by a finite or by an infinite system, she noted

does this bring us back to maximal being? he asked

it does bring us back to *What is God?* she replied
attempts to explore the question must use humility
we have to mind the chains that bind us to earth
as the Apostle has explained to us: *what God is*
no material being can know but the Spirit of God

it is easier to describe what God is not:
God is not an object in the material universe
God is neither a spatial nor a temporal being
God is not a contingent being

while we cannot fully comprehend what God is
we can contemplate logical propositions about God
we say with confidence: His essence is His existence
while other things receive existence God is existence
we hold God's properties are identical to each other

why is this? he wondered

forgive me, she said, i have moved too fast

maximum concern involves prayer and supplication
therefore we are invited to communion with God
to grasp that which we cannot we think of God as having
properties such as loving, forgiving, and being merciful
but God does not have properties in the same way
as creatures have, instead God is Her properties
God's properties are not distinct from one another
His Mercy is His Love, Her Love is Her Forgiveness

the Doctrine of Divine simplicity, he remembered

the very one implies that God does not change in time
for change is a modification of one property to another
but all real properties of God are the same, she explained

God's immutability follows from God's simplicity
God's knowledge and God's power are identical

while God's actions are not in time their consequences
are temporal or atemporal, God wills the unchanging reality
the numbers, the books, the libraries, the Platonic Forms

are all atemporal objects necessary existents? he asked

things that are contingent are so by the will of God
things that are necessary are so by the will of God
the underlying realm is coeternal with God, she said
yet God is the only One whose essence is existence

God is the One without a second
God is the only One who is truly necessary

she paused

i can never stop marveling at this library
she exclaimed, the books delight my heart
the cathedral of infinity inspires my awe

why is everything built of books? he asked

the library arises from the Eternal Word
the foundation of the soul is the Logos
the soul enables us to know what is Good
the soul enables us to love what is Good
the soul is both the knower and the lover
but knowledge and love are given to us

a library is a manifestation of language
a library is a temple instantiating a mind

I·5

is the existence of God self-evident? he asked

the philosopher has said the existence of God
is self-evident in itself but not to us, she replied

the essence of God is beyond our understanding
the creation cannot fully comprehend the Creator
what is outside of God cannot encompass God
only the highest thought finds the highest content

nous noesis, he reflected

Her existence is Her essence, she continued
there are limits in us we cannot overcome
and one consequence is that absolute Truth
can be contemplated but not comprehended
She can be loved, She can captivate us
She resides within us but She is beyond us

She? he wondered

God has no gender, she explained
does God exist? does Existence exist?
does Logos exist? does Truth exist?
does Love exist? are the same questions

since God is that which exists does anything else exist?
empirically the answer is *yes*, she pointed to the world

why does she draw on empiricism now? he wondered

but is there anything that exists independently of God?
to that question the devout answer is *no* since another
independent existent would diminish God's greatness
but God is maximally great! beyond Him is no other

God does not create out of necessity but freely
God is ultimately free and entirely unbounded
God is Existence Herself and Goodness Herself
God is Love Herself and Truth Herself

God is not identical to any particular notion
of truth we might be able to entertain now

since Truth is a substantial property of God it follows
God is not above Truth instead God is His own Truth
God is His own Existence, God is His own Goodness
God's Goodness is Her Love, God's Love is Her Truth

ultimately it is very simple, she said, and beautiful!

is God a person? he wondered

this particular direction is a prominent approach
sprung from revelation and sanctified by great love
but to think of a personal God is not the only way
because God's grandeur is above all our perceptions

in some theistic traditions God is thought of as a person
but this does not mean a person in the human sense
God is not a person as in having a limited personality
God is so different from what we normally consider
a person that i often worry the term confuses people

in early discourses of Christianity conducted in Greek
the term was *hypostasis* which means *underlying state*
but from Greek to Latin *hypostasis* became *persona*

the translation was famously upheld by the philosopher
who thought it fitting to call a rational hypostasis a persona
usually we are well advised to concur with the insights
of the *Doctor Angelicus*—i rarely find reason to deviate
every single page he wrote can be seen as a miracle

God is a person in the sense that we are invited to love God
to pray to God, to be with God, to devote our lives to God
we are invited to think of God as our lover and our beloved
but God can also relate to us as a parent, sibling, or child
God offers a loving relationship suitable to every soul

they continued to walk in silence through the library
then returning to his original question, she remarked

the existence of God is not self-evident because
we observe that some people construct worldviews
which assume that God does not exist
such perspectives usually generate inconsistencies
but those are not immediately obvious to all
it may take time and reflection to see them

those worldviews which are formulated with sincerity
have to be embraced respectfully and studied patiently

ultimately there will be a mathematical theorem
stating that worldviews without God are inconsistent
then we have a choice between God and inconsistency

as of now we can formulate the conjecture
that all arguments against God's existence
can be shown wrong based on reason alone
but proofs for the existence of God are
not tight enough to replace the gift of faith

faith is meant to be important in this life
since our response to God, our love for God
should come from a position of free choice
we have but this one life to live by faith

they walked on

if you are guided by Love you will conclude
that the existence of Love is self-evident
and you will understand that God is Love!

later on she said: theism is not the only worldview
but the only one that has a possibility to be consistent
since consistency is desirable for a rational enquirer
theism is the one worldview that can be embraced
while insisting on rationality

i genuinely admire your conviction, he replied
but could you explain the terms that are used here

theism means to be open to the existence of God
worldview is a theory that describes what exists
how our knowledge arises, and what our purpose is
rationality is a principled preference for consistency

1.6

shall we enter the coliseum of mathematics? she asked
they stood before a structure resembling a Platonic solid
its twelve transparent faces were perfect pentagons

with great delight, he answered, why is it a dodecahedron?

Plato proposed God used this solid to arrange the heavens
also the architect had a sense of humor, she explained

once they entered another surprise awaited them:
the grand foyer projected to them as a dodecaplex
the four-dimensional analog of a regular dodecahedron

slowly rotating it inverted within and beyond
making volumes unbounded and confines disappear
the geometric sway permitted the interpretation
that the entire library was enveloped by mathematics

what an ingenious design! he exclaimed

they call this room C120, she replied highly amused
some consider it an affront but others a masterpiece
of instructive geometry and timeless architecture

the theme is repeated as we delve into the library:
dimensions expand and perspectives transpose
pursuant to conjecture the library's innermost room
is an infinite dimensional sphere which contains
the whole world and is contractible to a point

along the endless corridors leading from the foyer
in all 720 directions they noted long blackboards
which displayed handwritten notation and drawings
in some places writings on the wall were in the making

it is the path to truth that matters not only the result
she explained, because mathematics is eternal learning

below the transparent floor on which they were walking
he perceived circles that were hastily drawn in the sand

noli turbare circulos meos! she commented

originals? he wondered

preserved for eternity and now undisturbed by war
she replied in the affirmative as he assumed

the idea is to record how evolving temporal thought
finds mathematical certainty that is impassable
exploration happens in space while truth is beyond time
mathematical truth is discovered but not invented

let us find rooms which individuate ideas, she proposed

they entered a complex plane that contained many papers
in addition to an extensive number of ever-present books

we may encounter unproven conjectures, she said
picking up a random paper and handing it to him

Über die Anzahl der Primzahlen unter einer gegebenen Grösse
he read its promising but somewhat archaic title

a coincidence? she wondered

i don't think so, he replied

all agree that primes were created by God, he added
even if everything else was a human invention

all who know? or all who do not know? she asked

among primes order emerges in the aggregate
although individual numbers can be eccentric
there is really nothing random among them
yet probability is used by ambitious analysts

does mathematics lead us to God? she asked him

mathematics leads us to God, he asserted

discovering mathematics happens in places
but mathematical truth is eternal and ubiquitous
mathematics points toward an immaterial realm
mathematical truth is Truth—and Truth is God

a widespread confusion which arises at times
is the view that the material world is all there is
that reality is exhausted by material phenomena

analyzing this view you realize it cannot be defended
because some abstract concepts must be permitted

but the view stipulates that those abstractions
are only our own constructs, our own inventions
they may include numbers, sets, shapes, love...

what is love for a materialist? she wondered

how would i know? he answered, i am a realist!

what is love for a realist? she pressed the point

everything! he exclaimed, since love is for beauty
mathematics reveals the realm of breathtaking beauty
you are persistently aware of her and you realize
that she will never pass (he was certain of that now)
but for materialists abstract objects derive from matter
they represent concepts which are invented by us

can Truth be invented? she asked

materialists tend to deny Truth with capital T

how can a view be true that denies Truth? she wondered
(diligently capitalizing her T)

the view severs us from God because the material realm is
presented as all there is and God is not a material object

if materialism is correct where is God? he continued
then God did not create people but people created God

already Plato and Aristotle agreed, she reminded him
that to be is not the same as to be material

materialism corrects those lovers of wisdom, he replied
for materialists a human being is a collection of molecules
that are working together obeying intricate laws of nature

are those laws not mathematical objects? she wondered

if nothing existed other than matter then a human being
is not more than a molecular machine, he contended

within that machine there is no one who knows
there is no one who thinks, no one who decides
all actions just happen according to laws of matter
arguably augmented with the spice of randomness

there is a field of phenomena but there is no knower
the view accommodates no God, no i, no you, no others
but do not think of Buddhism because there is no rebirth
there is no transcendence, no enlightenment, no dharma
there is no ferry that can bring you to the other shore
—there is no other shore

the life of an individual, the lives of all humans
the lives of all animals and plants, the entire universe...

yes? she asked

...become void of purpose! there is no purpose!

materialism leaves us empty and without purpose
each day we awake anew to the same nothingness
the god of materialism is nihilism

can the view evaluate its own consistency? she asked
because the view itself resides beyond the material

i agree that materialism is self-defeating, he replied
but a materialist might answer as follows:
the view is a consequence of the material world
an independent evaluation does not exist
and therefore cannot be required

but is "a consequence of the material world"
not an immaterial object? she wondered

i guess it is, he said

to reject materialism—if that is your desire—
you need a single immaterial point, she said

give me that point and i move the world for you! he replied

does mathematics offer you that point? she asked

it does, he answered, it most certainly does
it does in the stance of mathematical platonism

this position is defined by three statements:
i. there are mathematical objects
ii. mathematical objects are abstract
iii. mathematical objects are independent of humans

if mathematical platonism is correct
then materialism must be false, he continued

we are not pitting science versus mathematics
while science studies the material world
materialism is not a position implied by science
materialism is not part of the scientific method

instead materialism is a philosophical choice
it is a worldview, a metaphysical position
i expect that many scientists would accept
mathematical platonism on deeper reflection
but the question is: can it be proven?

the three propositions are called
existence, abstractness, independence

abstractness is unchallenged: mathematical objects
are abstract because they are not spatiotemporal
if they were spatial then mathematicians would
search for their locations similar to biologists
who find organisms or species in certain places
if they were temporal they would come and go
there would be a lifetime associated with a number
we might witness the birth and death of groups
or the emergence and extinction of families of sets
but mathematical objects are atemporal, not in time

then we can grant *abstractness*, she said

the mathematician and philosopher Gottlob Frege
developed a decisive argument for *existence*

Frege made the observation that the singular terms
of mathematics purport to refer to abstract objects
Frege said a sentence is true if it succeeds in referring
but for success to be granted the referent must exist

consider the sentence: "13 is a prime number"
this sentence can only be true if 13 exists
if 13 did not exist then how could it be true?

Frege's next point was: we agree that in mathematics
those sentences which are called theorems are true
we accept that mathematicians know what they are doing
when they announce that a proposition has been proven

hence Frege established *existence* of mathematical objects
although the argument seems decisive it has been countered
since the critics do not deny the idea of mathematical truth
in order to challenge Frege's argument they have to be artful

those philosophers who reject mathematical platonism
posit a distinction between a mathematical language L_M
and a separate philosophical language which they call L_P

consider the sentence S: "there are prime numbers"
they grant S is true in L_M but "S is true" is a sentence of L_P
while "S is true" is true in L_P, S itself is not part of L_P

thus the masters of L_P can comfortably refuse to accept
that prime numbers exist but still admit that "S is true"

philosophers are resourceful, she said with admiration
although i wonder if the tactic could be questioned

the challenge denies the existence of mathematical objects
L_P supposedly does not refer to mathematical objects
but L_P does refer to L_M which is a mathematical object

furthermore i think that L_P is less understood than L_M
as formalism of L_P improves it will become similar to L_M
ultimately only varieties of mathematical languages remain:
$L_{M1}, L_{M2}, \ldots$ and each one is committed to abstract objects

as our understanding of the world improves all languages
that can be evaluated will be of a mathematical nature

turning a corner they now perceived endless waves
of books extending in all directions toward infinity
what is revealed in those volumes? he wondered
the mathematics of everything, she answered

if we side with Frege, he continued undeterred
we have established a position called *object realism*
which recognizes both *existence* and *abstractness*
hence there exist abstract mathematical objects

object realism may not defeat all versions of materialism
especially not those that permit some abstract objects
if they derive from material ones and are reducible to them

to reject this extended materialism we need to insist
on the third point which is *independence*:
mathematical objects are independent of humans

toward this end consider the counterfactual statement:
if no humans were present in the material realm
there would still exist abstract mathematical objects

this argument is accepted by many analytic philosophers
who are those that embrace the tools of mathematics

mathematical truth is discovered but not created by humans
if a mathematical statement is proven its truth value becomes
known to us but the truth value is fixed prior to its discovery
and it has not been altered by the proof that is given

we can formulate a stronger version of *independence*:
mathematical objects are independent of any events
or phenomena that could occur in the material world

it is natural that we appeal to truth in mathematics
without the need of any empirical observation
a proven theorem demands no test within matter
mathematical truth is independent of physics
it is independent of chemistry or biology

mathematical truth determines what happens
in the material world but remains unaffected by it

mathematics is immaterial, eternal, unchanging
in that sense mathematics leads us to the Divine
mathematical truth emerges from Divine Truth
mathematics reflects the Beauty which is God

by God's creative choice the world is mathematical
by God's mercy we understand some mathematics
we see some of the order that permeates the world
the tools of mathematics enable us to study the divine

only now they realized that from their position
they also had a view of the ocean of truth
it extended serene in the golden afternoon sun
without a single sail breaking its emerald surface

is the ocean also part of the library? he wondered

the ocean flows in and out of the books, she replied
if you stand here at night you gain the impression
that the entire universe with its stars and planets
with galaxies and voids is mirrored in the ocean
and is therefore also present within the library

but remember my curious friend, she continued
mathematics, science, philosophy are never done
they will never reach the end of their endeavor
and this is another indication that we are placed
into a world which is upheld by an infinite God

MOVEMENT
2

.

next to the great library was a magnificent garden
countless corridors flowed from one to the other
even to knowledgeable visitors it was unclear
where the library ended and the garden began

the garden was glorified in the books because its
many blossoming forms infused the written word
thus garden and library were intricately connected
one was within the other together they were one

in her considered opinion the union established truth
one recorded the word while the other grew the form

the organic symbiosis between garden and library
was another masterpiece of the celestial architect
a celebration of eternity which she knew was not
a succession of moments but a limitless present

she walked in the garden following winding trails
among flowers and trees, pastures and woodlands
along ponds and brooks arched by bridges of jade
in the distance blue hills sloped into white mountains

often she found places she had not seen before
marveling at forms whose shadows were cast
for a first time upon any material instantiation

sometimes she decided to bring with her books
from the library, then she enjoyed reading them
under the canopy of trees on warm summer days
or among the drifting leaves of a colorful autumn
or in the clear moonlight of an everlasting spring

she felt that those books were talking to her
intoning sublime harmony of effulgent wonder
over the years they had become her friends
some told her of worlds that were far away
others sang of universes that resided within

the garden was inhabited by a diversity of species
her loving eyes observed parents raising their young
there were fawns playing with their joyous siblings
there were cygnets and peachicks partial to her

in the morning mist or in the evening twilight
appeared occasionally the silhouette of a unicorn

once she had read that all animals had obeyed Noah
when he called them into his ark but not this one
confiding in its own strength it declared i will swim!

weighing forms and their instantiations she wondered:
who lifts potentiality into actuality? who forges ideas?
who moves time? who fixes the canopy of the stars?
who weaves the fabric of the universe guiding souls?

she called the vibrant nature the garden of philosophy
because here she was one with the ideas themselves
in comparison other places she had seen and admired
were present to her rich memory as mere shadows

the garden and the great library were open to all
their gates stood ajar but few people noticed either
although exploring them was the purpose of life
according to the perennial philosophy she cherished

she was ready to walk through the garden of wisdom
with everyone who was looking for her in life

                              ❋ ❋ ❋

one day in early summer a conversation unfolded
along the living walkways and paths of the garden

as you can see, she began, in the grounds of philosophy
God permits many seedlings to blossom for our delight
around us are countless species of roses, camellias
lilies, tulips, peonies and together they manifest
rich compositions of intense color and fragrance

gymnosperms and angiosperms enchant this habitat
where they cooperate and thrive in peaceful harmony
therefore i conclude that many astonishing varieties
appear to be acceptable to our master gardener

but permit me to remark, he said with ardent devotion
both for the garden and for her who walked beside him
that Plato's theory of Forms is the mainstay and pride
of the horticultural collection that appears before us

incorrigible realists see the same flower everywhere
she said laughingly, because their desire is one-pointed

since everything sprouts from the soil of the garden
even those who disagree with the food must take it
the devoted realist of all existing Forms remarked
we see dissenters wandering through life aimlessly
until in the end they return to their place of origin

the odyssey of philosophy is decidedly a painful one
we have the urge to call out to our friends: hurry home!
do not lose the spur of unchanging light! he continued

where is home? she asked gazing at a cedar of Lebanon
whose branches bowed gracefully in the morning sun
and who can give them a swift ship of the Phaeacians
that is steered by thought and never misses its mark?

what a fitting remark! he said, for in Plato's perspective
the physical world is less real than the realm of ideas

i must admit that i find great comfort in this, he added
the hint of something greater than mere material existence
is persistently revealed to us every single moment of life
what appears to our senses is an imperfect image of reality
it is a shadow of an underlying, unchanging, perfect sphere

walking in Plato's garden what is it you see? she asked

his ideal realm is populated by forms which are unchanging
they are the immaterial and timeless essences of all things
objects of the material world are imitations of the forms
while the forms alone provide meaning and understanding

the highest kind of knowledge which is attainable to us
is the noble intuition of the forms themselves, he added
although we can never know any one form perfectly
knowledge of instantiated objects is even harder to gain

she listened with delight as he continued with fervor
Plato deduced that we can know more about universals
than about individuals—knowledge of the latter is only
possible since they participate in the underlying forms

Plato uses the terms *Form* and *Idea* interchangeably
the Greek words for them being *eidos* and *idea*

Plato was not first to note the problem of universals
already Thales of Miletus who was a mathematician
and presocratic philosopher formulated the question
if appearances change what is it that is changing?

the answer which Thales gave was *substance*
but that proposition leaves us with a new question
how does an object or thing relate to its substance?

at this juncture Plato seeds the garden of philosophy
which flourishes so magnificently around us today

a Form or Idea answers to the question: what is that?
what is a flower, a tree, a garden, an animal, a human?
what is love, courage, hope, beauty, humility, goodness?

what is a Form? she added to his list of examples

precisely! he exclaimed with great excitement
Platonic Form is another example of Platonic Form

the garden and her presence inspired him to persevere
forms are the proposed solution to the problem of universals
how can one thing in general be many things in particular?

Plato's insight teaches us, his devoted students, to discern
between the many objects that appear to us as beautiful
and the one object that is what beauty is, that is beauty

you are aware of her presence without being able to hold
on to her although she is neither elusive nor mutable

beauty is not in a person nor in an animal
she is not in a sunset nor in a line of poetry
she is neither in heaven nor on earth
she is not in one thing nor in another
she is just by herself and with herself

but she is before me now, he thought
and her lure is mistress of my will

suddenly he paused . . . she continued calmly
the task of a philosopher is to discover through reason
the underlying nature of forms and their relationships
this activity will culminate in an understanding
of the most fundamental form: the form of the Good
if he is patient he will gain what he is looking for

but tell me, my friend, she said, what did Plato think
about the relationship between a thing and its form?

material objects participate in the forms, he said
a material object is a table if it imitates the form table
a better table is more successful in doing so
but no instantiated table is ever the perfect table
no instantiated flower is ever the form flower
a form is the objective blueprint of perfection

again arose that poetic longing in his voice

a form does not belong to any particular person
her eyes seemed to word with loving compassion

take the geometric form of a triangle, he continued
a teacher draws a triangle on the blackboard before
her attentive students: but however great her skills
at drawing, the image will not be a perfect triangle

she cannot produce entirely straight lines which are
infinitely thin and meet in three immaterial points
she does not teach the imperfections of a drawing
but instead she professes the perfection of a form

if the lesson succeeds an understanding of the form
is passed from her mind to those of her students

but the form itself remains perfectly unmoved
whether or not the students comprehend the lesson
at the end the drawing is erased but the form stays

a material triangle is both a triangle and not a triangle
instantiation prevents it from being a real triangle
only the form itself is just a triangle and nothing else

you take away everything that is not the form itself
until you attain that which is the form and nothing else

if you ask me to provide that which is just beauty
and nothing else then you request the form itself
if i ask you to reveal to me that which is just you
and nothing else then i request of you yourself

they had reached a place in the park where statues
stood under tall trees and between them were ponds
in one pond glided serenely the form of a swan

is this the legendary swan of Saraswati? he wondered
if you offered him a mixture of milk and water
then he can drink the milk alone

she too was in thoughts as she looked at the swan
was intuition of certain forms present within her?
did she remember them from a previous life?

tell me more about those forms, she demanded

consider the form Large, he said, this tree is large
this tree is an individual, largeness is a universal
the property *large* can apply to many individuals

this tree may be larger than many other plants
but it is small when compared to a mountain
every individual that is large is also not large
while the form Large is truly and only large

this is one of the aspects that distinguishes
individuals and universals, objects and forms

for Plato it was evident that forms are not
invented by us but they are discovered by us

knowledge is based on forms, not on instantiations
individuals we know via forms in which they partake

we know because of forms, because of universals
but our knowledge of forms is never complete
we may never fully understand a particular form

not in the confines of the material world, she thought

Socratic dialogues examine forms but never gain certainty
Plato never offered a complete description of any form
we are left wondering over gaps which need to be filled in
Plato himself and others after him criticized the theory

Plato does not claim to understand the mechanism
by which material objects participate in the forms:
how does a form appear in many objects?

Plato does not provide us with a list of all forms
he does not explain what is a form and what is not a form
how many forms are there? infinitely many? countable?

Plato said that mud or hair were so irrelevant that they
did not deserve to be forms, he added for amusement

most of Plato's works are dialogues in which people ask questions
Socrates is the main teacher who entices people to think carefully
then he analyzes their answers, accepting some, rejecting others
then he asks new questions—in the end he gives the best answers

but in one book a young Socrates debates an aged Parmenides
here Socrates criticizes the forms and is in need of education

we never know for sure what is Plato's own opinion
is Socrates always presenting Plato's perspective to us?
or is he proposing an idea which Plato does not fully accept?
which insights are Socrates's and which come from Plato?

when Socrates died Plato was 25 years old
Plato lived to reach an age of more than 80 years
many dialogues are written long after Socrates's death
it is unlikely that Plato offered only Socrates's ideas

Aristotle was Plato's student but he never met Socrates
while Socrates did not exert himself to leave any books
both Plato and Aristotle generated for us vast corpuses

Plato's works are preserved but Aristotle's published books
were lost in temporal turmoil devoured by bookworms
only his terse lecture notes written for himself survived

Aristotle wrestled with Plato whenever he found a chance
he was respectful but challenging, he disagreed if possible
Aristotle founded his own school years after Plato's death
Plato is dear to me, he told his students, but dearer is truth
Aristotle is seen by many as a more practical philosopher
but personally i would never trade realism for practicality

the Socratic problem is the question: who was Socrates?
what were his teachings and opinions? was he focused on
ethics alone or did he engage ontology and epistemology?
it seems we will never know unless we encounter Socrates
alongside Plato or Aristotle walking in this beautiful park

she was now inclined to sit down in the garden under trees
she wanted to read a book she had brought from the library
she invited him to stay near her and he gladly accepted

resting in the warm grass anticipating to fall asleep
he resolved to contemplate only that which she was
being silent in her presence he began to comprehend
that eternal happiness was forever getting to know her

and then in his dreams she enlightened Socrates
who was a good student about the nature of love
seeing them in conversation it occurred to him
that they represented both instantiation and idea

on a blank slate which stood before some benches
that were arranged under tall trees in the garden
they found four lines inscribed by a graceful hand

1. Beauty exists independently of human thought.
2. Beauty exists as a form in beautiful things.
3. Beauty is a mental construct in our brain.
4. Beauty is a name but nothing is Beauty itself.

is our teacher offering knowledge in this garden?
i wonder what she is up to now? she asked

what a fine way to instruct in the midst of nature
which is fragrant with the perfumes of spring
what an elegant handwriting is revealed here
oh how i wish to be in her class! he exclaimed

be careful what you wish for, she joked
what if you were unable to meet expectations?

i would strive to do my very best, he said

what if your best was not good enough? she teased

i hope no effort would satisfy entirely, he replied

is this your idea of heaven? she asked

a philosopher given a choice between going to heaven
or hearing a lecture on heaven must choose the latter!
sadly this one here seems to have ended, he added

or is about to begin, she remarked

can you enlighten me about the writing? she asked

she is teaching four ways for interpreting reality, he said

are these the only four? she asked

i would not claim that they are exhaustive
but they are certainly four crucial ones
they represent: *realism, immanent realism,*
conceptualism, and *nominalism* in sequence

let us discuss them in turn, she proposed

what a delight! he replied

realism is Plato's perspective that abstract objects exist
but they dwell neither in time nor in space, he began

abstract objects are not material, not mental, not passing
they reside independently of us in a Platonic heaven
which is neither a physical place nor a temporal structure

abstract objects include properties and relations
being beautiful is a property as we have discussed
but beyond beautiful flowers, beautiful gardens,
and beautiful trees, there is also beauty itself

beyond all trees is the property *being a tree*
beyond all elephants is the property *being an elephant*
if elephants became extinct—what a worrying thought!
the property of being an elephant would still persist

in addition to properties relations are abstract objects
larger than, south of, student of are relations
elephants are larger than mice, Sparta is south of Athens,
Aristotle is a student of Plato who is a student of Socrates

in addition to relations, propositions are abstract objects
ver erat aeternum and *Es war ewiger Frühling*
are latin and german sentences for the same proposition

❀ ❀ ❀

in contrast *immanent realism* is Aristotle's perspective
that numbers, properties, relations, and universals exist
but they are within material objects of the physical world

to a pile of three books add one to get a pile of four books
in this way numbers are manifested in the material realm

the property *being red* is in red flowers and red sunsets
for immanent realists if all red objects were to vanish
from the physical universe redness would no longer exist

Aristotle agrees with Plato that knowledge requires forms
but for Aristotle those forms must inhere in matter

in his extant lecture notes Aristotle denies three times
the independent existence of Platonic forms

❊ ❊ ❊

conceptualism argues that properties or universals exist
but they are mental objects which reside in our brains
the view is also called *mentalism* or *psychologism*

beauty, truth, or numbers become mental constructs
they are neuronal firings in the brain of the beholder

❊ ❊ ❊

nominalism holds that there are no abstract objects
numbers, properties, universals are only names

there are piles of three books but no number three
there are red flowers but nothing itself is redness
redness is only a name, rose is only a name
man has the ability to name! man is only a name!

nominalism is only a name! nominalism is anti-realism
nominalism argues against the real existence of forms
amusingly nominalists agree with the following statement:
if there were numbers they would be abstract objects

❊ ❊ ❊

they resumed walking through the splendid garden
which for realists existed in an unchanging reality
that was independent of any human activity
while for immanent realists it existed in matter
while for conceptualists it existed in their brains
while for nominalists it did not at all exist

let us focus on numbers as placeholders for properties,
universals, relations, and propositions, he suggested

for Platonists numbers exist as abstract objects
for immanent realists numbers exist as physical objects
for conceptualists numbers exist as mental objects
for nominalists numbers do not exist, they are names
(but if they were to exist they would be abstract objects)

the lines are drawn, the world is divided, the armies are ready
all four perspectives have devout followers among philosophers
who have thought deeply and sincerely about those questions

platonism is embraced by many philosophers and mathematicians
among them we can find Russell, Quine, Frege and Gödel

Willard Van Orman Quine? she wondered

. . . was a Platonist when it came to mathematical objects, he replied

in favor of platonism Plato offered the one over many arguments:
this flower is red, this tree is red, this roof is red, this sunset is red
since those objects have something in common *redness* exists

it is a good start, she said

hold on! nominalists interject, we accept sentences of the kind
this flower is red, this roof is red, but we deny redness exists
you Platonists have never really explained to us what redness is
for us redness is a red herring, we claim that it does not exist

then Quine enters and says: nominalists deny redness
but they accept the sentence *this flower is red*
we note that herein *this flower* is a singular term

in simple sentences we are ontologically committed
to objects referenced by singular terms, Quine says

Platonists and nominalists agree that the sentence
this flower is red is true and therefore both agree
that the object *this flower* exists

nominalists and Platonists accept Quine's notion
of ontological commitment

but now the ground is prepared to argue for platonism!
the argument is Frege's who said: if a simple sentence
is true then the objects denoted by its singular terms exist

Frege continues: many simple sentences are literally true
and refer to abstract objects—hence abstract objects exist
the sentence *seven is a prime number* is literally true
therefore seven exists and by extension numbers exist

Frege offered compelling arguments against mentalism
according to Frege it is evident that mentalism cannot
account for truth in mathematics—here are four reasons:

1. theorems about numbers cannot be evaluated by mentalism
because we cannot have infinitely many number ideas in our head

2. theorems about large numbers cannot be evaluated by mentalism
because if no human has ever thought of such a number then
that number would not exist

3. if all humans were to disappear the statement *3 is greater than 2*
would become untrue

4. whether a prime number exists between two large numbers
would be an empirical study to see if such a number is in our brain
clearly this is not a proper method for finding truth in mathematics

Platonists accept we have ideas of mathematics in our heads
but deny that mathematical theorems are about those ideas

mathematics also provides arguments against immanent realism:
the concept of a mathematical set is not about physical stuff
sets are not simply collections of physical or material objects
sets can contain other sets, sets can be infinitely large
with many sizes of infinity reaching far beyond integers

there is no plausible way how set theory can be construed
as a theory of physical stuff—the universe of sets does not
consist of hadrons or quarks or photons or gravitational fields

mathematical Platonists usually convince other philosophers that
immanent realism and conceptualism of mathematics are untenable
the remaining dispute in the philosophy of mathematics occurs
between Platonists and nominalists, that is realists and anti-realists

the latter are hard-pressed to refute Frege's singular term argument
and all attempts to do so require certain strange contortions which
leave us stranded in nowhere land in my entirely unbiased opinion

but nothing in philosophy is ever settled, he admitted with a sigh
philosophy is lingering discourse, perpetual learning, ongoing life

from the benches of beauty a quiet path had led them
under tall trees along a running brook to an open field

why is lingering discourse present in philosophy
but not in mathematics? she wondered

both are moved by love for beauty and for truth
neither will ever reach the goal of their endeavor
neither will be done, neither will ever find home
what makes them differ? what makes them similar?

for now the one is focused on underlying *eternalia*
while the other is confused by material sensations
once this difference between them disappears
the two disciplines will become one field of study

elsewhere in the garden on a piece of parchment
resting on a stone table the same gracious hand
had written down a column of five propositions

1. Mathematical objects are not in space and time.
2. Human beings are entirely in space and time.
3. Thus human beings cannot attain mathematical knowledge.
4. Human beings have mathematical knowledge.
5. Thus mathematical Platonism cannot be correct.

i am certain that this is not our lady's opinion, he exclaimed

how can you arrogate to know her sentiment? she countered

i wish to think that our teacher has written those propositions
as an exercise for her students to analyze and to refute them

if this was the case, she said, and you had the privilege
to be among her students then how would you proceed?

her students must be advanced since this famous objection
has engaged learned philosophers in extensive debates

her students may be beginners in the matters of life
but perhaps not in the ways of philosophy, she offered

what she has formulated here, he explained, is known as
the epistemological challenge to mathematical platonism
epistemology is the celebrated discipline of knowledge

the question is how can we know abstract forms?
if Platonic Forms do not reside in the material world
how do we access them in order to know them?
the teacher has focused on the mathematical arena
but the same objection can be raised to all of platonism

what would be the reply of a renowned realist? she asked

implicit here is the notion that forms are causally inert
that abstract objects cannot cause events in the world
if they cannot cause events they cannot induce knowledge

a realist may challenge the view that forms are causally inert
if they were how could mathematics govern material events?

by declaring abstract objects as causally inert, he continued
philosophers limit themselves to a particular view of causality
which only applies to interactions between material objects

some realists may prefer an extended notion of causation
admitting interaction between abstract and material things

adopting a temporal perspective we can say
abstract objects move or guide material events
adopting an atemporal perspective we can say
material events are in synchrony with abstract objects

let us ask: how did Plato propose to solve the problem?
Plato thought that humans consist of body and soul
and the latter has knowledge of abstract objects
the soul remembers forms from a previous life in heaven

i like the idea that we hold memories of heaven, she said
how do mathematicians solve the problem? she asked

Gödel thought that humans have a mathematical instinct
which is an abstract object and has access to abstract forms

Plato's and Gödel's suggestions rely on the idea
that abstract objects interact with material ones
because Plato's soul interacts with the body
and Gödel's instinct interacts with the brain

now we see the necessity for the remark on causation
but in addition we realize that both Plato and Gödel
saw humans as more than purely material objects

if we adopt this perspective then proposition 2 is invalid
and the argument falls apart or is inconclusive

a materialist assumes that everything humans do or think
is a consequence of chemical events occurring in the brain
to challenge that position we can ask what happens
in a class when a teacher explains the form of a triangle

we ask what is transmitted? what causes students to learn?
how does the teacher's brain modify that of the students?
beyond material brain states there are immaterial thoughts
beyond material notation there are immaterial referents

if abstract objects are present in the knowledge of humans
they are part of us, they are part of what it is to be human
we are what we know, we become what we learn

i love Plato's and Gödel's attempts, she said, because they
lead us to the point where the temporal and atemporal meet

where is that? he asked

within, she replied

he reflected on her words and they were silent
then he asked her, is our lesson finished for today?

not quite, she answered, turn over the piece of parchment
he did and found three statements written on the other side

1. Mathematical objects are not in space and time.
2. Human beings have mathematical knowledge.
3. Thus human beings are not only in space and time.

as you can see the challenge to platonism has become
an argument questioning materialism, she said

the argument is acceptable to a realist, he said
but i wonder what others might make of it

would you like to challenge it? she encouraged him

adopting the role of detractor i formulate as follows, he said
consider a smart computer with mathematical knowledge
it is programmed to find new theorems and does so at times
imagine it surprises human mathematicians with its ingenuity
imagine that the computer can also formulate new conjectures
and engage with experts to discuss open mathematical problems
humans may credit the machine with mathematical intuition
it may surpass the best human mathematicians in some aspects

the computer is built of semiconductors, it has a motherboard,
central processing units, graphics processors, memory cards,
it has power supplies, cooling devices, a support structure
it stands in a particular place and operates at a specific time

can you say this computer is not a purely material object?

she replied, imagine an algorithm that factorizes primes
or an algorithm that provides the digits of our beloved pi
or even a very simple algorithm for sorting numbers
are those algorithms material objects? she asked

they are not, he said, they are mathematical objects

very good! she replied, your computer, which is imagined
for now but may be instantiated one day, contains many
algorithms and on inspection they are abstract objects
can the computer operate without them? she asked

it cannot, he replied

then the computer is not only a material object
while it is in time and space it is more than that
do you agree? she asked

now i do, he said

the computer is both material and immaterial
seeing the computer as purely material is incorrect

knowledge is an abstract object, she continued
the activity of knowing is an abstract object
but it is not only the problem of knowledge
which brings us in touch with abstract objects

elementary particles obey mathematical laws of nature
therefore seeing them as purely material is confounded
every material object that is guided by abstract objects
is itself an abstract object to some degree—i propose

being guided by abstract objects is an abstract object
being touched by abstract objects is an abstract object

may i ask how you define abstract object? he said

abstract objects are not in time and not in space
abstract objects are immaterial and timeless

can abstract objects be agents? he asked

they can, she replied

can abstract objects be patients? he asked

they cannot, because they are unchanging

he looked at her

it is misleading to see elementary particles, planets
cells, brains, computers as purely material objects
if you do so you realize only half of their nature

whatever is material is touched by the immaterial
whatever is in time is touched by timelessness

God holds every atom and every moment in existence

does evolution bring us to God? she asked one evening
as they were sitting in the garden under scintillating stars

evolution does bring us to God, he responded at once
from the very origin of life via increasing complexity
evolution led to bacteria, archaea, plants, fungi, animals
then among animals evolution brought forth hominids

homo sapiens could as well be called *homo spiritualis*
because from our beginnings we have searched for God

evolution has equipped us with a trait that sets us apart
from all other animals: this trait is human language
using the tools of language and its thought processes
we promptly turn to God and ask questions about God
we wonder about the world and about us in the world

empirically we conclude: evolution has brought us to God

does evolution necessarily lead to creatures that seek God?
she wondered looking at the stars which were above them

the same chemistry holds anywhere in the universe
therefore on planets with conditions similar to this one
it is possible that origins of life occur, he answered
then life unfolds according to the laws of evolution
and evidently this process is able to find intelligence

let us define intelligent life as that which has traits
that are equivalent to human language
we can use the word *iLife* for those organisms
that have the ability to make infinite use of finite media

if *iLife* is present on a planet it will detect abstracta
it will see the eternal realm and query transcendence
it will ask philosophical questions and wonder about God

evolution brings forth realists and rationalists
evolution unearths anti-realists and nihilists
evolution brings to light mathematicians and scientists
poets, composers, architects, engineers and saints

evolution discovers lovers of wisdom
but those who love wisdom love God
thus evolution finds lovers of God

if i asked you to define human language, she said

she was looking at the contours of the great library
which were illuminated by the light of a silvery moon

to this end permit me to attempt as follows, he replied
human language is a tool of unlimited expressibility
utilized for combinatorial thought and communication
it weaves material brains into communities of seekers
thinkers, researchers, problem solvers, writers, dreamers

its quasi-unlimited potential is a most relevant feature
unlike animal communication which contains a few signals
human language generates an infinitude of expressions

we can ask fortuitous questions, explore hypothetical scenarios
seek counterfactual statements and employ logic to aid reason

language gives us access to mathematics and to science
language is discrete infinity—from a finite set of words
it produces unlimited quantities of sentences and books

infinity matters, she thought, because God is unbounded
and so is the world of forms and the realm of mathematics

the laws of chemistry and physics permeate the universe
the same laws of biology apply universally, he continued

if the right compositional matter is present on a planet
then evolution can perform its art, it can bring about iLife
which in turn searches for truth, for wisdom, for God

there are a billion planets like earth in our galaxy
which is just one of one hundred billion galaxies
that populate the observable universe which in turn
may only represent a small fraction of the whole universe

there are 10^{20} planets like earth in our field of view
and perhaps many more beyond the horizon
on many of those planets could be ongoing evolution
sometimes leading to iLife which falls in love with God

thus love and prayers emerge from the laws of physics,
of chemistry, and of biology anywhere in the universe

there is an ordered hierarchy: physics enabling chemistry
chemistry enabling biology, biology enabling evolution
evolution leading to language, language turning to God

the hierarchy itself emerges from mathematics because
all laws of nature originate and reside in mathematics

without mathematics the laws of nature would not exist
material processes following those laws would not exist
mathematics is a formal cause for all physical processes

God is the formal cause too, but also the efficient cause
and the final cause, she added looking again at the stars

stars come in many different sizes, he continued
their lifetime is inversely correlated with their size
larger stars are short lived, smaller ones are long lived

for most of their life they fuse hydrogen to helium
but toward the end they run out of hydrogen
then they fuse helium into carbon and oxygen
and other elements that become useful for life

biological organisms consist of chemical elements
which were produced by those aging stars
stars in heaven are responsible for life on earth

star formation is a consequence of gravity and other forces
hence the forces of nature cooperate to produce the matter
which is used by evolution to weave the intricacies of life
the very forces of physics lead to beings who love God

how beautiful is the world in which stars seed
the universe with prayer everywhere, she said

he was silent

does evolution bring us to God? she asked one morning
sitting on a terrace overlooking the lush garden of forms

evolution does bring us to God, he affirmed once more

as life originated in the ocean after the stardust had settled
so life emerges in the truth of unfailing mathematical laws
the process of evolution points to an underlying reality
thereby rebutting a worldview which relies on matter alone

what can you tell me about the process of evolution? she inquired

evolutionary biology studies the unfolding of life
as it happened on earth over a period of four billion years

the field explores events that occurred over time
it aims to understand which organisms emerged
and what causes triggered change and innovation
it dates fossil records and analyzes speciation

some aspects of evolution are akin to historical studies
the goal is to figure out what happened when and why

evolutionary biology also wants to find reasons
for changes which took place in the trajectory
it seeks to understand whether certain novelties
were adaptive and why they arose at that time

evolutionary biology wants to know the likely causes
for the birth of new species and the demise of old ones
it examines bursts of radiation and mass extinctions

what caused the Cambrian explosion 541 million years ago?
what led to a world of dinosaurs 225 million years ago?
what triggered their decline some 60 million years ago?

but there is also another aspect to the discipline:
the term *evolution* refers to the mechanistic process
that causes living systems to change over time

the basic principles of the process are astonishingly simple
but from this simplicity emerges enormous complexity

we find that the laws of evolution are mathematical
biology rests on mathematics as do physics and chemistry
this is the amazing beauty of the material realm:
as atoms and stars follow the unchanging laws of nature
which are mathematical objects so do living organisms

it is via mathematics that evolution brings us in touch
with underlying eternal reality, with an absolute truth
the fundamental laws of evolution are abstract objects
which reside neither in time, nor in space, nor in matter

but they are—religiously—followed by populations
which are firmly instantiated in time and in space

since evolution points to an eternal realm, it brings us to God

tell me of those mathematical principles of evolution, she said

evolution occurs in populations of reproducing individuals
which can be cells, viruses, bacteria, or other organisms

cells contain genomes which encode information
during cell division the genome is duplicated
typically cells divide into two daughter cells
each daughter cells gets one copy of the genome

imagine one cell situated in a favorable environment
it has access to energy and to chemical compounds
it can maintain its structure and replenish its molecules

most of the energy for life on earth is provided by the sun
stars not only seed life, they also nourish it once seeded

cells have evolved mechanisms to capture this energy
which is then used to assemble organic compounds
the important process is called photosynthesis

let us return to our cell in the suitable environment
one cell divides into 2, 2 into 4, 4 into 8, and so on
this is exponential growth: 1, 2, 4, 8, 16, 32, 64,...

let us suppose our cells divide once per day
each day the population size is multiplied by two
in a year we would have 2^{365} cells which is a number
dwarfing that of atoms in the observable universe

exponential expansion is powerful and fast
it swiftly reaches the limits of any material ecosystem
those limits imply that our cells run out of resources

to add some realism we now include cell death
population growth is governed by birth and death
if birth exceeds death we still have exponential growth
but it will take a bit longer to reach the limit
if death exceeds birth we have exponential decline
which means the population becomes extinct

if birth balances death the population size is constant
often birth rates decline as population sizes increase
because then cells have greater difficulty to gain nutrients
in this case population size may reach a stable equilibrium

now imagine two different types of cells in competition
A cells divide into A cells, B cells divide into B cells
if A cells reproduce faster than B cells then over time
they become more numerous than their competitors
eventually the A cells will dominate the population

this fundamental principle is called *natural selection*
faster reproduction wins over slower reproduction
more efficient reproduction wins over less efficient one

the rate of reproduction is called *fitness*
fitter individuals win over less fit ones
natural selection leads to survival of the fittest
but there are many exceptions to this rule

if reproductive rates depend on relative abundance of types
then coexistence between types is possible in a population
the type that is fittest by itself may not exclude all others
in those cases natural selection does not maximize fitness

since birth and death occur according to probabilities
stochastic effects arise in population dynamics
therefore fitter types have only higher chances to win
evolution becomes a matter of chance and probability

natural selection means there is a contest to get better adapted
to the environment, the ecosystem and ever-present competitors

Darwin and a few others discovered evolution by natural selection
Darwin and Wallace read Malthus's book on exponential growth
which made them realize the power of exponential expansion
then they concluded that nature could act as a gigantic breeder

Darwin did not conceive of any mathematical equations
in fact he regretted not to have the intuition to do so
but those equations came later as it was realized that
the process of evolution was mathematical in essence

it became evident that a precise understanding of evolution
is not possible without a mathematical formulation

similar developments had occurred previously in physics:
Copernicus placed the sun in the center of the solar system
but Newton's equations of gravity explained what that meant

he paused

natural selection is only one part of the story, she said

you are right! he replied, we need to ask what causes
different types to emerge and the answer is: *mutation*
selection and mutation are the two pillars of evolution
in the classical description of the process

let us return to our simple cells: their genome is instantiated
by a long molecule called Deoxyribonucleic Acid or DNA
DNA is a string of nucleotides, it is a biological polymer
its sequence encodes the genetic information of the cell

mutations are random alterations of the sequence
for example one nucleotide is replaced by another
or some nucleotides become deleted or others inserted

the stochasticity of molecular reactions leads to mutations
a mutation once made can remain in the genome of the cell
and be passed on to daughter cells—mutations are heritable

while advantageous mutations increase the reproductive rate
disadvantageous mutations reduce it and neutral mutations
leave it unchanged—most mutations in genomes are neutral
those neutral mutations can accumulate by random drift

Darwin did not know the details of the mutational process
these insights were obtained later by building on the work
of Gregor Mendel, a monk with mathematical intuition

mutation generates variation while selection acts on variation
both mutation and selection follow mathematical laws

i guess we are not done, she remarked

then there is also *cooperation*, he said

biology is not only built on the principle of competition
we find that cooperation is ubiquitous in all domains of life

cooperation means biological structures help one another
cooperation entails paying a cost to benefit another individual
cost and benefit are measured in terms of reproductive rate

the idea of cooperation seems counterintuitive: why should
organisms help their competitors in the struggle for survival?
yet cooperation occurs on all levels of biological organization
in fact cooperation is instrumental in generating those levels

cooperation occurs among genes, cells, organisms and people

a living cell is the product of cooperation among genes
multicellularity arises from cooperation among cells
animal communities are built around cooperation
human language emerged as a consequence of cooperation
among people who were negotiating their place in society

cooperation—not competition—is the master architect
of the evolutionary process that unfolds life on planets
more than competition, cooperation is the force that makes
life what it is, that leads to increasing complexity over time

in summary, we may be permitted to conclude as follows:
mutation generates variation upon which selection can act
mutation and selection produce living matter that cooperates

cooperation adds a silver lining to a world that is violent
cooperation is a preparation for love which is the purpose of life

whenever we study the wonders of evolution
we observe everlasting, unchanging principles in action
we are led to the realm of underlying timeless reality
we are led to something that is intrinsically divine
we are led to God!

... there is grandeur in this view of life

if the process of evolution is based on randomness
are its outcomes uncertain? she wondered

let us keep in mind, he said, that all natural events
occurring in the material world are based on randomness
the most accurate mathematical formulations of physical
chemical or biological mechanisms utilize probability
the fundamental basis of all natural law is randomness

stochastic descriptions of scientific processes are
more precise than their deterministic counterparts
the latter represent useful approximations

in quantum mechanics the Schrödinger equation
describes a wave function and the square of that wave
is the probability to find a particle in a certain place

the molecular motions of thermodynamics are random
with probability being the main consideration of entropy

chaotic dynamics is a feature of nonlinear equations
that are ubiquitous in nature and especially in biology
simple deterministic rules can give rise to behavior
that is complex and unpredictable

while some stochastic processes can be predicted
certain deterministic ones cannot

but randomness and unpredictability do not imply
the absence of all conceivable structure
randomness does not void the laws of nature
but fulfills them! randomness obeys mathematics

even in a world that is based on randomness
we can understand science and find our bearing
we can build bridges, tools, machines, computers

although molecular motion is based on randomness
materials tend to have very consistent properties
and chemical reactions occur in reproducible ways

although evolutionary dynamics use randomness
many aspects of the process proceed as expected
the fate of some mutants can be very foreseeable
evolution of resistance to vaccination or treatment
often arises according to mathematical certainty

but it is an open question to what extent evolution
operating on a geological time scale is predictable
if evolution on earth were to unfold a second time
would it find the same structures and organisms?
would there be DNA, RNA, proteins, lipids, cells?
would we have elephants, mice, zebras, humans?

evolutionary biology will be able to answer this question
once we see instances of life emerging on other planets
perhaps one day—after having encountered thousands
of planets flourishing with life—we may conclude
that evolution on a planetary scale is rather predictable

there may be similar origins of life on distinct worlds
there may be unfoldings which roughly proceed from
simple cells, to higher cells, to complex multicellularity
evolution may find the equivalent of human language

we must remember that evolution is a search process
mutation, selection, cooperation explore possibilities
that exist within a vast space that is being searched
this space is given by the mathematical laws of nature

whether or not the evolutionary processes that occur
on different planets are very similar or very distinct
depends on the constraints within the search space
both the space that is being searched by evolution
and the process of evolution are Platonic Forms

i appreciate, she said, that randomness is the tool of choice
for the scientist observer who is caught in the flow of time
the fact that many natural laws are based on probabilities
does not constitute an argument against divine providence

God operates in all processes that occur in the material realm but since God resides outside of time the entire trajectory which is lifted by Him into existence is present before him

events that appear random in the realm of secondary causes are not random with respect to primary and final causation

time arises from the fact that everything outside of God
is attracted by the love of God and thus on a course of change
time is the ordering of motion, the logical sequence of effects
that we encounter in a creation which is on the way to God

books may depict people as walking through the library
they provide an image of time but the library is timeless
the library and the garden of forms rest unchangeably within

at the foundation of physics we find conservation of energy
as a principle that follows from the time invariance of laws
physics which describes motion is based on timelessness

know that time loops from atemporality and returns to it
the material and the abstract are two sides of one essence

God is that one essence, she continued

from God comes the pair: temporal and atemporal
material and immaterial—God wills them inseparable

Plato pointed to heaven and Aristotle to earth
but in doing so both philosophers indicated God

lovers of wisdom often err on one side or the other
either they give too much or else too little emphasis
to that which is material and to that which is ideal

as if real existence resided in only one of the two
but in fact we know that God wills them both

the ideas of the garden, the books of the library
live forever in the mind of God but a single moment
of instantiation is infinitely valuable to Him too

do not search for the one in what comes from the One
because only God is One, what descends from God is Two
without One there is no Two, without Two there is no time
unification of all knowledge and existence is in God alone

do not think that temporality is followed by eternity
instead eternity is in every moment, eternity is now

eternity transcends time, eternity is manifested
in dreams when asleep, in thoughts when awake
in the embrace of a beloved, in the smile of a child
in the gentle breeze moving the leaves of the garden
in the pages of books or on the waves of the ocean

eternity grounds your existence and holds your essence
the totality of love you offer is present in every moment
what you were before the beginning of time you still are
what you will become at the end of time you are already

she was carried away for a moment and then fell silent

as the silence descended he thought
before i knew her there was time
when i am not with her there is time
when i am with her there is no time
what does this make her?

MOVEMENT
3

she went out into the villages to teach students
they knew not who she was but saw what she was
she reached their hearts and transformed their lives
she sent them on journeys that would not falter

she taught them in poorly heated classrooms
on those grey days when shelter was needed
when rain hammered unabatingly on windows
when winds swept over the barren landscape

she taught them on meadows or in forests
on those beautiful days of calm tranquility
when the sun ushered in a mild season
or refused to abandon a golden autumn

devoted classes were invited to visit her
she met them in rooms of the grand library
or in the celebrated garden of philosophy
which flowed from books into the world

then they sat around her in the tall grass
or on benches under the canopy of trees
that shaded against the heat of the day

whatever their chosen meeting place was
the students eagerly awaited her arrival
and they listened to her fully focused
with that boundless curiosity of youth

as the years passed in the material realm
steadily she became a teacher of all people
bringing about what was called a golden age

❀ ❀ ❀

we are continuing our passage through time
she told her students one day in late summer

our recollection has reached Aurelius Augustinus
at the threshold of antiquity and the middle ages
in biographies he is portrayed as the last man
of the former and the first man of the latter

from the ancient teachers Augustine inherits
the idea that philosophy is the love of wisdom
Augustine agrees with Plato that the philosopher
is a lover of God because wisdom is identical to God

he does not distinguish between theology and philosophy
they are intertwined and Christianity is the true philosophy
he provides sharp arguments against those perspectives
that are materialistic in essence and distract from God

he is influenced by Platonism and Neoplatonism
which provided him with tools to analyze the world
but he faults them for arrogance because they assumed
they could reach happiness by their own virtuous effort
—for Augustine arrogance is the main reason of failure

Augustine's declared program is to make progress
toward knowing God and toward knowing the soul
for this endeavor he combines Platonic philosophy
and biblical revelation into a single worldview

since Augustine is a Platonist we find that
many of his ideas are Platonistic in nature
permit me to list some examples for you

1. The unchangeable is above the changeable.
2. The Forms reside in the mind of God.
3. God is immaterial yet causally present in the creation.
4. Sense experience differs from knowledge.
5. What can be known is within.
6. Within we find God and Truth.
7. The soul is immortal and incorporeal.
8. The soul loves God out of erotic desire for beauty.
9. Evil is privation of goodness.

she wrote down each statement on the blackboard
which was before them in the garden of philosophy
those propositions link Plato and Augustine, she said
they establish a firm continuity which i admire
i want you to think about each of them in turn

※ ※ ※

Augustine develops the idea of intellectual ascent
which happens when we turn inwards toward our soul
when we move from the sensible to the intelligible

transcending ourselves we encounter the Supreme Being
which is more central to us than our innermost self

this Supreme Being is God

beyond Atman is Brahman, beyond Brahman is nothing
resounded in the memory of one her students

Augustine agrees with Plato that God is the first principle
that God is the supreme good and the reason of knowledge
but he thinks we cannot reach happiness by our own efforts
instead it is accessible only by mediation of God Incarnate

✳ ✳ ✳

Augustine's theory of knowledge is his doctrine of illumination
he thinks that true knowledge requires first-hand acquaintance
while second-hand information yields at best justifiable belief

in the case of sensible objects—which do not admit knowledge
but only opinion—acquaintance arises through sense perception

cognition of intelligible objects cannot be reached empirically
nor be transmitted linguistically by a human teacher
rather such cognition requires our own intellectual activity
which we judge by a criterion that we find within us

examples of this cognition are mathematical or logical truths
which we understand only once we see them for ourselves

this theory of Augustine is called *Divine illumination*
because God is present within our soul as a teacher

as the sun is visible and illuminates visible objects
so God is intelligible and illumines intelligible objects
the former are seen by the eye the latter by the soul
thus God instantiates reason which is the eye of the soul

Divine illumination is an alternative to Plato's recollection
how does Plato think we know the forms? she asked

according to Plato we know forms by remembering them
from a previous life in heaven, one of her students replied

in contrast for Augustine we know the forms, she continued
because they are illumined by God, our teacher and creator
for Divine Illumination falls within the framework of creation

our mind is created by God to be connected to reality
we see intelligible objects in light of truth which is God
every human being is illuminated by the Divine light
and therefore can pass judgment about right and wrong

yet to develop those intuitions and lead a virtuous life
we need to turn to God who is the source of all light
while human beings are able to access intelligible truth
only those will succeed who have sufficiently good will

we must remember that the striving for wisdom occurs
in a world that is subjected to confusion and failure
thus the true understanding of God can only emerge
after this earthly exile when we see Him face to face

for Augustine faith is needed for all understanding
crede ut intelligas—believe so you may understand!

on the temporal journey faith is prior to understanding
a first step to perfection is to believe the words of scripture
the next step is to realize that those words are outward signs
which lead to an inner truth—again we find Truth within

* * *

Augustine contributed to philosophy of language
he differentiated between the sound of a word
the meaning of a word and the object it signifies
language is a system of signs used by speakers
in order to signify what they wish to express

he thought that we do not learn things from signs
for in order to understand the meaning of a sign
we must already know the thing that is signified

he solves the problem with inner teacher and illumination
he often refers to an inner world which resides within us
the inner world is generated when we activate a kind of
latent or implicit knowledge that is present in our mind

Augustine concludes the inner world is not linguistic
instead it is atemporal and goes beyond language
since it is not formulated in any particular language
the theory of the inner world is not a linguistic theory

may i remind you that universal grammar is not
a grammar but a theory for a set of grammars
which is learnable by the human brain

(that remark stood alone in the motionless air)

❀ ❀ ❀

Augustine thinks that a human being consists of
body and soul with the latter governing the former

the soul is the life-giving part of the human being
the center of consciousness, of perception and thought
the rational soul controls sensual desires and passions
the soul becomes wise by turning to the Supreme Good

in his Manichean phase prior to his conversion in 386
Augustine thought that God and soul are material entities
but his Platonist readings gave him philosophical tools
to envisage a world that contains immaterial realities

at this time he developed his famed hierarchy:

1. God is immutable and immaterial.
2. The soul is mutable in time but not in space.
3. The body is mutable in time and space.

the soul is of divine origin and god-like
it is not divine itself but created by God
he defines soul as a rational substance
that is empowered to rule over a body

he thinks the soul is incorporeal and immortal
and can in principle exist without the body
which again resembles Plato's perspective

he thinks that immortality of the soul can be proven
by philosophical means but ultimately he fails to give
a convincing proof according to his own evaluation

immortality is necessary but not sufficient for happiness
true happiness is realized in the eschaton as a gift of God
when not just the soul but the whole human being lives forever

for Augustine resurrection is not susceptible to a rational proof
it is God's promise that must be believed on scriptural authority

due to his Platonic view of soul he inherits a classical problem:
how does an immaterial soul govern a material body?

❋ ❋ ❋

Augustine thinks the mind is created in the image of God
because it has the potential to become wise and to love God

since God is the greatest good our desire for happiness
can only be satisfied by God alone: *happy is he who has God*
to have God means to know God and to love Him

we are virtuous if we turn to God—virtue is love that
knows its priorities while vice perverts the natural order

we pursue some goods for their sake and others for greater ones
he says: enjoying a thing means to love it for its own sake
using a thing means to love it for the sake of another thing
which we want to enjoy—we love absolutely what we enjoy
while our love for things we use is relative and instrumental

he knows that the only proper object of enjoyment is God
again he attributes this idea to his Platonistic predecessors

confusion of moral order is reversal of use and enjoyment
when we want to enjoy what we should use—all created things
when we want to use what we ought to enjoy—that is God

do we enjoy our neighbor or use him? a student wondered

what is your own opinion? she asked him in return

my poor intuition suggests the former, he answered
but Augustine's teaching seems to recommend the latter

Augustine is aware of the problem, the teacher replied
he cautions us against talking of using human beings
true love between humans is mutual enjoyment in God
love of neighbor means to desire her true happiness

we must avoid the misunderstanding that we can enjoy
a human being without reference to God, for this would
mean we expect to receive from her our true happiness
which no human being can provide but only God

❀ ❀ ❀

virtue guarantees happiness as it is oriented toward God
but virtue itself comes to us as a gift of God's grace

what are the four cardinal virtues? she asked her students

they replied: temperance, prudence, justice and courage

those four are subdivisions of love, she continued

Augustine interprets the biblical command to love God
and to love your neighbor in terms of Platonic Eros
as we have learned from the teachings of Plato and Plotinus
we also hear from Augustine: *love is a force in our souls*
that attracts us to true beauty which we find in God alone

love moves us to ascend from the sensible to the intelligible
and from there to the cognition and contemplation of God

love indicates for us the direction of our will

sin arises as misguided self-love which is equivalent
to pride and puts the self in the position of God
in contrast legitimate self-love strives for true happiness
by subordinating the self to God

every action even those that seem just can be motivated
by good or by evil intention, by right or by perverse love
take care that your inner disposition behind your activities
is love of God and of neighbor instead of self-love or pride

❀ ❀ ❀

Augustine teaches us that the ideal agent is a stoic sage
who acts out of inner virtue, rationality, and true love
but adapts his outward actions to external circumstances

since love and will belong to the privacy of the mind
the inner motives of a person are unknowable to anyone
except the person and God—this view which i endorse
limits our authority to pass moral judgments over others

here i agree with Augustine who repeatedly recommends
that we should withhold judgment to preserve our humility

he thinks that our inner motives are opaque even to ourselves
they are transparent only to God, thus we can never be sure
about the purity of our intentions or if we will persist in them

all humans are called to examine their inner moral state
continuously in a prayerful and humble dialogue with God

❀ ❀ ❀

Augustine introduces the concept of will to philosophy
he describes will as the faculty of choice within the mind
will is related to love, will is a place of moral evaluation
we act well or badly if we are driven by right or wrong love

will is our inner consent for which we are responsible
sin is the will to pursue actions or longings that are unjust
will must be freed by divine grace to be able to resist
mundane temptations which may even haunt the saints

grace restores our freedom but does not constrain our will
Augustine teaches us that original sin transformed
our initial ability not to sin into an inability not to sin
divine grace restores our ability not to sin in this life
and transforms it into an inability to sin in the next life

❀ ❀ ❀

Augustine rejects the existence of evil as a substance
he endorses the Neoplatonic view that evil is unsubstantial
he sees evil as privation or corruption of goodness

a created being can be said to do evil if it falls short
of its natural goodness because of sinful corruption
but even in that case only the corruption is evil
while the nature of the being itself remains good

Augustine claims that the seemingly simple question
what causes evil will? is unanswerable for us now

❀ ❀ ❀

his theology of grace is central to Christian teaching
he thinks that human beings in their present condition
are unable to will the good by their own efforts

freedom of choice has been damaged by original sin
and must be liberated by grace to develop the good will
which is necessary for true virtue and happiness

he paints the city of God in contrast to the earthly city
criterion of membership in either is right or wrong love
people in the city of God direct their love towards God
people in the earthly city love themselves more than God

true happiness which is sought by every human being
cannot be found outside the city of God

❀ ❀ ❀

Augustine contemplates hostility, aggression and revenge
he concludes that war results from sin and lust for power
a just war has to be waged for the benefit of the adversary
without any vindictiveness but out of love of neighbor
it is evident that just war is utopian in a fallen world
the same conclusion holds for punishment or revenge

❀ ❀ ❀

concerning the philosophy of time Augustine teaches us
that God does not create in time but creates time together
with changeable beings while resting in timelessness Himself

creation occurs instantaneously: the seven days of creation
are a didactic tool to make plain the intrinsic order of reality

similar to Plato's demiurge God creates out of goodness
out of gratuitous love for His creation and all that exists

Augustine proposes in creation all three hypostases are active:
the Father accounts for existence, the Son for form or essence,
the Holy Spirit for goodness and orderliness of all creatures

God creates formless matter out of nothing—that is *ex nihilo*
He imprints on it the rational principles which exist in His mind

3.2

in the garden of philosophy she taught her students
under the hanging branches of a cedar of Lebanon
there was an arrangement of benches and chairs
on a blackboard was drawn the figure of a triangle

not only a triangle, she said, but every geometric form
every shape, manifold, or curve is a Platonic object
every proposition, every theorem, every derivation
every algorithm, every number is a Platonic object

the celebrated universe of sets is a Platonic object
every thought, every idea, every group of thoughts
every composition of ideas is a Platonic object

human discoveries including the wheel, the lever
or the game of chess point to Platonic objects

every book in the great library is a Platonic object
ideas in the garden of philosophy are Platonic objects
both the library and the garden are Platonic objects

not only the form chair but this particular chair
which has been made with love is a Platonic object

the sunset ahead of us and its serene redness
which follows the golden hour are Platonic objects

every moment of the temporal trajectory
and the idea of a moment are Platonic objects

elementary particles are Platonic objects
and so are the fundamental forces of physics
the chemical elements are Platonic objects
and so are the molecules they assemble

cells, plants and animals are Platonic objects
the process of evolution is a Platonic object
and so are natural selection and random drift

a student was anxious to ask a question
he had tried raising his hand several times
but had not been courageous enough to do so
in the end it happened almost involuntarily

at once she paused to acknowledge him

may i ask what is not a Platonic object? he said

your question is much appreciated, she answered
it is a recurrent enigma among lovers of wisdom
some say that a satisfactory answer does not exist
it may be the case that the set of Platonic objects
is recursively enumerable but not its complement

one attempt is to argue that those compositions or acts
which do not partake in eternity are not Platonic objects
events that are not illuminated by the Form of the Good
have no place in eternity and are not Platonic objects

what has no presence in God's mind is not a Platonic object
but who are we to conjecture what is present in God's mind?

we may argue: since evil is not a substance, evil acts should
not remain eternally but God can bring good out of evil
we may propose that everything which is not compatible
with the Love of God will be passed over in timelessness
but what is incompatible with the all-embracing Love?

i think that certain aspects of evil deeds will be forgotten
for love keeps no record of wrongs as the Apostle has written
but again i argue for caution because our minds cannot grasp
what it is that has no place in the thoughts of the Most High

does this help for now? she wondered

of course, Madam! thank you! the student replied

he fought for composure when she spoke to him
it was not easy to maintain eye contact with her
being known by her lifted him among the elect

he was relieved when she turned to look at others
then he wondered if they had similar experiences
he would never know since he could not ask them

he listened with curiosity when others spoke of her
when they expressed their admiration and love
but he never participated in those conversations
he considered it inappropriate to talk about her

that day something lasting happened in the encounter
she had placed a Platonic object into his heart
which one? he wondered as the lecture continued

every temporal instantiation has something fleeting
but no composition in time is entirely impermanent
every instantiation is both fleeting and permanent

every material object contains something eternal
but often it may be indiscernible to us what that is

when i say this chair is a Platonic object i mean
it contains something that is a Platonic object
since God is innermost existence in all that exists
there ought to be a Platonic object in all things

God is not a Platonic object i hasten to add
God is above Platonic objects as their creator
as their primary cause and their final cause

considering two chairs i propose that both participate
in the same universal chair which is a Platonic object
but each one of them also contains its own Platonic object
each one is crafted by a different love and is willed by God

what is willed by God is illuminated by the Good
everything contains the eternal blueprint of what it is
we can say that individuals participate in universals
but both individuals and universals are eternal objects

Platonic forms reveal the architecture of the world
they interlink time and eternity, matter and mind
Plato's insight was to realize the intricate connection
between the world of change and unchanging reality

Plato built a bridge between Parmenides and Heraclitus
between being and becoming: on one side all is in flux
on the other side what is is and what is not can never be

she stood up and walked among the students
who were seated in the garden of philosophy

everything that partakes in being is a Platonic object
what we call Platonic object we may call eternal object
for those eternal objects i like to use the term *eternalia*

Plato may argue only some of them are Platonic objects
but i cannot see that subset, i am unable to do so

it is probably a moot point albeit of historical interest:
had Plato been aware of the ability of mathematics
to grasp all aspects of the world in being and becoming
he may have widened the scope of his category anyway

she paused, are there any remaining questions?

can the garden of philosophy prove its own consistency?
a student asked whose thoughts were often in the clouds

i do not see a finite number of axioms defining philosophy
thus limitations of finite systems may not apply, she replied
(because no finite system can prove its own consistency
as she and the dreaming student knew for a fact of logic)

does the garden only contain objects that point to God?
another student asked after a brief moment of silence

thoughts of God are from God and directed to God
the garden contains that which is willed by God
which is illuminated by God and points to God

she waited to see if there were more questions
since there were none for now she concluded:

awareness of eternalia eases the path to Truth
it provides a proper frame for interpreting reality
it kindles a Love which will never stop burning
it helps you to discern the graces that will prevail

3·3

the teacher and her students met in a room of the library
which offered perspectives of both garden and ocean
the windows were open admitting a mix of fragrances
and of light that bounced from the waves and leaves

she called those rooms *bridges* as they connected worlds

how does the atemporal rule the temporal? she asked
how do we know forms? what knowledge of ideas is in us?
can abstract objects causally interact with material brains?
which guardrails make matter obey mathematical regularity?
how do forms govern the unfolding trajectory over time?

how do forms specify which events occur in the material realm?
how do laws of nature constrain what happens every moment?
which principle breathes forth the logos that pervades the world?
what brings properties to individuals and universals to particulars?
does the Form of the Good illuminate all forms and all events?

those questions converge to one: what bridges the two realms?

giving them time for reflection she walked to a window
beyond majestic trees she saw blue mountains in the distance
above them was a morning sky not obscured by a single cloud
somewhere in those mountains resided the elated monastery

she turned and continued

when hydrogen clouds undergo gravitational collapse
they obey rules staked out by abstract objects
when the star dust seeds combinatorial chemistry
when prelife initiates repeated origins of life
when evolution leads to organisms of complexity
the material world diligently follows mathematics
which is laid down in the unchanging reality

later evolution discovers beings who are equipped
with the ability to learn about those natural laws
their mental activities are guided by them
they reason from them, they reason to them,
they reason within them, they reason about them

as waves and particles follow laws of physics
as living matter follows laws of evolution
so human thought follows laws of language

in all of those processes is an interaction
between material and abstract objects
material objects obey mathematical rules

material phenomena trail unchanging ideas
time follows that which is timeless
space follows that which is non-spatial

while the instantiated obeys the abstract
the abstract is free of the instantiated
temporal truth comes from absolute Truth
but absolute Truth rests in itself

she paused again

matter is in touch with abstract forms
so is evolution, so is human reasoning
the interaction between the material world
and the atemporal realm pervades all levels

elementary particles, celestial bodies, living cells,
and animal brains are guided by abstract objects

here is the answer to the questions that are before us:
underlying reality is the atemporal part of creation
the material world is the temporal part of creation
the two realms are intertwined, embracing each other
one is not without the other, together they are one
they are a manifestation of divine thought and action

some students wrote down notes

the Divine in His Love has granted us cognitive abilities
which allow us to study both the material and the abstract
therefore the material world appears to us mathematical
therefore we see the inexplicable efficiency of mathematics
therefore we perceive the logos which illuminates the world

here we find the meaning of the term *continuing creation*
since God is reliable we trust that the physical world continues
to behave in obedience to unchanging mathematical laws

God is the primary cause of all, God is the final cause of all
God permits secondary causes which are real and meaningful
secondary causes include laws of nature and choices of souls
which reside in the atemporal but are movers in the temporal

our souls move our bodies as laws of nature move matter
both matter and thought follow mathematics thereby linking
a changing material world to an unchanging immaterial one

our scientific understanding which is of mathematical nature
points to the fact that the world is ordered by divine thought
science points from matter to God revealing the form of reality

the atemporal is Divine Thought, the temporal is Divine Action
the connection between the two realms is Creation

since Creation is ordered by Divine Thought, the temporal
follows the atemporal, the material follows the abstract

Creation happens outside of time but its consequences are in time
God's continuing Creation of Love holds every instant in existence
it connects time to timelessness, matter to form, moment to eternity

there was a secular age and movement in the world
which made God less prevalent in the hearts of people
it followed progress in science but that was not its cause
for science removes superstition and counters false idols
if gods are used to explain that which science cannot
then as science advances those gods are needed less

scientific progress questions illogical concepts of gods
that might emerge at times but it does not argue
against the God of sacred scripture or of philosophy
it does not argue against the God of Plato, Aristotle
Plotinus, Augustine, Avicenna, Maimonides, Aquinas

now it is clear that science sharpens our view of God
that science is our friend on the journey toward God
but it was not obvious then in the age of confusion

it is difficult for us to understand the movement
you had to be immersed in the society at that time
the causes of the development were rather political
it was a rebellion against a dated world order
which was perceived as inflexible and intolerant

are you alluding to naturalism? a student asked

among philosophers this was the name used, she said
although *atheism* was the more precise description
because what unified the view was the conviction
there is no god and nothing that can be called god

it was further understood as the ontological commitment
that only that existed which could be studied by science
for this view *scientism* is a more accurate designation
while materialism or physicalism are related perspectives

in those particular attempts there is a material universe
populated with beautiful and astonishing phenomena
but the whole exists for no reason and toward no end

in the perspective of naturalism primary and final causes
are voided by metaphysical choice, not by scientific evidence

some thought science had brought them to this insight
but on reflection it had not because science by nature
only investigates secondary causes governing the world

while science does not study primary or final causes
philosophy has the imperative to do precisely that
therefore the scientific method which i admire
becomes incomplete when dealing with philosophy

naturalism undermined itself first because it had to admit
the indispensability of abstracta called upon by mathematics

mathematical analysis had been eminent in some areas of science
but as understanding grew mathematics permeated more fields
science became precise only when formulated in mathematics

the book of nature is written in the language of mathematics
the book of thought is written in the language of mathematics
the grammar of human language is a mathematical object

at that time mathematics spread from analytical philosophy
to philosophy in general, it reached all fields of study

is she talking about past or future? a student wondered

what is time between friends? she answered

she sat down on a chair on the patio of the library
the devoted students were assembled before her
it was the sacred hour of mid afternoon
they were facing the emerald ocean of truth

the consorts now offered them tea in porcelain cups
its fragrance was reminiscent of peaches of heaven
its taste was a harmonious variation of pure water
which had transported the evolution of life on earth

a consort placed a note on a small table next to her
she read it and nodded at the consort who withdrew

one of the students witnessed the fleeting interaction
because the consorts who brought tea blocked the views
of all other students but had left his open—by chance?

in that moment a daring possibility dawned on him
the inspiring teacher of this class, he conjectured
and the teacher of the world were the same woman
the idea captivated him for the remaining lecture

naturalism became an endeavor of mathematical investigation
every statement within naturalism drew mathematical notation
the attempt to give account of the world in terms of material
phenomena became mathematical, the teacher proceeded

and this ended the endeavor? one of the students asked

it gave pause to those willing to embrace depth, she replied

scientific progress, she continued, is oriented toward truth
but truth resides in mathematics, it is not a material object

science studies the temporal but rests on the atemporal
mathematics can be motivated by scientific problems
but mathematical truth is not decided by experiments

mathematical truth looms immaterial and atemporal
above and beyond all that is within time and space
science studies the consequences of mathematical truth
therefore mathematics is indispensable for science

as the centuries passed the great scientific method
celebrated for good measure as the best practice
had led in all domains of research to the realization
of a world which resides beyond time and matter

it had led back to God

at that time a view started to develop from the ashes
which was altogether not too different from ours
the view saw a directionality in the material world...

as in teleology? someone interrupted

or as in final cause, she answered

...according to which the nucleosynthesis in stars
seeded the universe with combinatorial chemistry
that instantiated beings which recognized the laws
upon which the material was built immaterially
from which the temporal flowed atemporally

science had recognized the much greater world
in which material universes are embedded
the atemporal world which points to the first
and final cause of all that is temporal and fragile

as is written in the books of the great library

in Thee abide fixed for ever
the first causes of all things unabiding
and of all things changeable
the springs abide in Thee unchangeable
in Thee live the eternal reasons
of all things unreasoning and temporal

science rejoined the first philosophy that studies the divine
not by revelation but through its effects, she continued
science recognized the immensity of divine truth and love
it was a move of reason toward healing a world in pain

naturalism was a term too beautiful to be abandoned
instead it changed its meaning for lovers of wisdom
it came to stand for a deep appreciation of nature
and of the scientific method which enables you to see
unchanging objects within the world of change
and unchanging beauty within passing time

the students began to see that the world around them
and within them reflected that unchanging harmony

be mindful, she said, all views emerging from pure hearts
are loved by God and are permitted to grow in His garden
they contribute to a diversity which is cherished by God

when we are caught in the flow of time we do not know
which flower will spring from an odd seed in the end

it is fine to argue for a perspective in humility
but the causes you are upholding must be God's
be careful whenever you critique alternative views
then you have to be able to argue them so well
that your discussants think you are holding them

always help others find what they are seeking
walk with them and your goals will cohere
avoid conflict because in this temporal setting
passions are confounded, judgement is obscured

do you understand me, my beloved friends?

some of them nodded but all remained silent

if i encounter people who have not opened their hearts
i do not consider it their failing but i examine my effort
evidently i have not succeeded in pointing out to them
the full implication of God's all-embracing love

i resolve to work harder to nudge them to open the door
my love reaches out to souls regardless of their trajectory

always remember, my friends, that the entire universe
of dispositions is dearly loved by God and has a purpose
every small flower sings the praises of God in her own way
those who do not know God today may find Her tomorrow

later she said

a teacher of wisdom has once declared: from souls
who do not see God we learn to do good for no reason

it is a remark worthy of reflection but i wish for you
to keep in mind that doing good is always for no reason

loving God means to do good as an end in itself
do not seek to collect treasures for yourself in heaven
instead be ready to stand before God with empty hands
then you can merge and become one with His love

how beautiful is this world that gives us the freedom
to move from individual love to God's universal love
how beautiful is this world that leads us into Her arms

3·5

a group of students approached her after class
what are we to think of the concept of soul? they asked

she recognized them as rather quiet students
who rarely asked questions but listened with dedication

in the Vedas, she began, *Atman* refers to soul
Atman is the true self, the essence of an individual
for humans to gain liberation they must know Atman

Atman who resides in every being is also *Brahman*
the soul of the individual is the soul of the world
the individual soul is likened to a drop of pure water
which eventually becomes one again with the ocean

for Plato, she continued, the soul is the source of life
the soul gives life to the body but it is also the mind
it is a mover and thinker, it moves itself and the body
it deliberates and rules, it is bearer of moral properties
Plato thinks we are virtuous if our soul is virtuous

Plato teaches that the soul consists of three parts:
logos, thymos, eros which are reason, emotion, desire

Plato assumes the soul is incorporeal and immortal
after the death of the body the soul continues to exist
and can think, it will be reborn in subsequent bodies

she paused

for Aristotle the soul is the first actuality of the body
it is the capacity to engage in the activities of life

Aristotle draws a hierarchy of such activities:
growth and nutrition for nutritive souls of plants
motion and perception for sensitive souls of animals
intellect for the rational souls of human beings

he thinks the soul cannot be separated from the body
the soul is a capacity, not something that has a capacity
it is the form of the body, it makes matter a living body

Aristotle argued the soul cannot exist without the body
but he was less certain whether the intellect could do so

could you please extend on this last point? they asked

in the fifth chapter of the third book of *De Anima*
Aristotle seems to suggest the soul itself is immortal
but some scholars think that the passage only refers
to the part of the soul representing the active intellect
Aristotle's real opinion however will never be known
since the text is ambiguous and he does not discuss
the point elsewhere in any material available to us

she paused again

for Augustine the soul is a special substance
endowed with reason adapted to rule the body
a human being is a compound of body and soul
within this compound the soul is the ruling part

the rational soul can control sensual desires
the soul has the ability to move closer to God
the human soul becomes wise if it turns to God

the soul is life-giving and seat of consciousness
the soul is mutable in time but not in space
the soul is not divine itself but created by God

when contemplating bodily resurrection Augustine said
it is natural and desirable for a soul to govern a body
but he renounces the classical idea that to be happy
the soul must free itself from all corporeal constraints

in agreement with Plato Augustine thinks that the soul
is an immortal substance which can exist without a body
immortality is necessary but not sufficient for happiness
true happiness can be realized in the afterlife when due to
the resurrection of the body the human being lives forever

for Aquinas human beings consist of body and soul
the latter is the principle of life actuating a body

human functions such as understanding and willing
are for Aquinas obviously not physical processes
they cannot be performed by material bodies alone
although they depend on bodily participation

we have intellect and will because of our soul
but it is not my soul which wills instead i do

Aquinas thinks when the body dies the soul persists
but the soul alone is not a complete human being
my soul survives my death but my soul is not me

Aquinas thinks the soul is the form of the body
and hence it is not perishable by natural causes

there is no logical proof for immortality of the soul
it survives the death of the body by the will of God
at resurrection the soul will be reunited with the body
because the soul naturally belongs to the body

Aquinas also states that all our natural properties
are present in Christ's risen body, she added

Noli me tangere, she thought

Descartes is a dualist who holds that humans
are composed of two substances: body and soul
Descartes thinks he is his soul and he has a body

for Leibniz the soul is a monad whose primary
and perhaps only causal interaction is with God
each soul holds the entire information of a universe
but in a way that is fully transparent only to God
since any aspect of the world affects the soul

all interactions that occur between souls are based
on the principle of a pre-established harmony
any conversation we conduct or any book we read
is written into our souls from the beginning of time

Kant considers the soul to be immaterial, she said
he does not hesitate to equate the soul with the I

Madam, which of the teachings do you embrace?
they asked after a respectful silence

i accept all approaches which are inspired by love
which spring forth from a pure heart, she replied

but to satisfy your curiosity i am happy to explicate:
the human person is a compound of body and soul
we are corporeal and spiritual beings willed by God

the human body is animated by a spiritual soul
which refers to or defines our innermost aspect
by which we are created in the image of God

the human body shares the dignity of the Incarnation
and therefore the whole human person is intended
to become a temple of the Spirit in the body of Christ

this is the teaching of the Eternal Word and therefore
it is also my view! do you follow me? she asked

Madam, we wish to follow you always! they replied

smiling at them who stood before her she continued
made of body and soul the human person is a unity
the elements of the material world are in our body
may we bring them to perfection by raising our voices
in praise and in love freely given to the Creator!

we must not despise our bodies but we are obliged
to regard them as good since God has made them
and will lovingly raise them up on the last day

the soul makes the material body a living human body
the union of spirit and matter forms one nature in us

the soul is created and willed by God to be immortal
it does not perish when it leaves the body at death
it will be reunited with the body at resurrection

now she was silent and they became aware
of the subsistent sound of the rolling ocean
and of the seagulls that populated its shores

do you have any further questions? she asked

Madam, what kind of body may we imagine here?

you may envisage a transformed body, she replied
since flesh and blood do not inherit the kingdom of God

the students left bowing to her respectfully
but one of them remained—suddenly he asked

Madam, if i have a burning heart is my soul on fire?

she looked at him

the spiritual tradition of the Church emphasizes the heart
as the depth of our being where we decide for or against God
it is a burning heart that connects you to heaven

when she saw that the other students had left she got up
then he who had been standing before her knelt down

why do you kneel before me? she asked

Madam, forgive me, but i know who you are

what makes you pronounce enigmatic words? she asked

my heart is on fire, he answered

his eyes were lowered, he did not dare to raise them anymore
although a few moments ago they had talked face to face

you may remind me of your name, she said

Nachiketa, he replied

that evening falling asleep in a stygian room of the library
she encountered an umbral memory from a remote past
on the heavy desk before her rested a large open codex
whose pages emanated words like vapor which she inhaled

the light had gone out and there was darkness
she had ventured into the realm of death
as her mother had sent her there in anger
she realized she had gone too far this time

she was afraid of the unknown
yet she found the place empty
how strange! she wondered
although patiently she waited

after three days Lord Yama returned
noting the unattended guest in his home
he was abashed by his lack of provision

my Lady, he addressed her formally
please forgive my failure to honor
the sacred obligation of hospitality
which is an imperative for all beings

to make up for my omission
and to substantiate my apology
pray let me offer you three boons
one for each night you waited

if i have fulfilled each of them
to your satisfaction, my Lady
and you will be the judge of that
then release me from my debt

she was pleasantly surprised
by the unexpected turn of events
his well refined manners helped
to calm down some of her fears

formulating her first wish she said
my mother has sent me here in anger
hence i beg from you, noble Lord
that she take me back on my return
please reestablish the fine harmony
which has always existed between us

consider it done! Lord Yama replied
he liked the kindness of her wish
and welcomed the circumstance
that very little effort on his part
was needed to grant this request

he began to entertain the hope
that he might get away cheaply
as economy mattered to him

and what is your second wish?
the Lord of Death asked expectantly

for a moment he even considered
lighting one of those fine cigars
but then he refrained from doing so
(we do not know if considerations
of health mattered to him at all)

after some deliberation she said
while all on earth fear you, my Lord
no one in heaven is afraid of you
therefore please teach me the art
that duly connects me to heaven
so i am able to teach others

i am pleased with your request
Yama replied, i will teach you

the fire ritual prepares the way
for it is a burning heart of love
that connects you to heaven
if your heart is on fire the link
is established the bridge is built

be who God means you to be
and you set the world on fire

if all your thoughts and actions
are illuminated by a burning love
then you are joined to heaven
you will be without fear of death

the ritual is performed variously
you can be a servant to people
or acquire proficiency in a craft
you can seek unchanging truth
or pursue activities celebrating
the light of beauty cast on forms

make all you do an offering of love
make all you do an offering to God
then you will lose the fear of death

if you love God you find God in all
if you love God you see the path
that connects all creatures to heaven

the fire ritual is the service of love
desire for that which is unchanging
speedily opens the gates of heaven

honor your parents, give alms to the poor
study sacred scripture, contemplate the absolute
participate in creation with a humble disposition

i hear your words, i sense their meaning
she replied, my heart is already on fire!
the love for the Most High consumes me

i am happy to hear this, my Lady, he answered
she who performs the ritual with threefold knowledge
who respects in gratitude mother, father, and teacher
who fulfills three duties, crosses over birth and death
she knows the wisdom that has sprung from eternity
unconfused she rejoices in the blessed sight of heaven

in silence she committed his words to memory

he resolved to inspect her more closely
he was drawn to the allure of living matter
the fragility of flesh and blood attracted him
he began to search for justifiable reasons
that would have permitted him to strike
but something about her made him hesitate

i beg you, my Lady, to request your final boon
he suggested returning to the business at hand

after some contemplation she said, all mortal beings
who ask questions wonder what happens after death?
the answer to this query is my third and final wish

my Lady, Lord Yama replied with a sigh
the answer to that particular question
was not even known to the sages of old
therefore release me from this boon

Lord Yama, you say not even the wise
know the answer to my third question
thus i conclude no greater teacher than you
can be found to enlighten my curiosity

Yama now realized that avoiding this third boon
might require him to reach deep into his pockets
which were substantial though economy mattered

what if instead i offer you glory and fame on earth
a long and pleasant life with countless descendants
that are equally blessed; in addition i give you wealth
beyond what the world has ever seen, herds of cattle
and of elephants, enumerations of swift horses,
chambers of gold and silver, ships that roam the sea,
lovers i bestow on you who will never disappoint!
i give you beauty of body and a lucidity of mind
which will never succumb to age or affliction
i make you Queen of earth and enjoyer of desires

my noble Lord, great is your power
that you can offer such mighty gifts
yet worldly pleasures tempt me not
they last but a day in face of eternity

as for ruling there will be another
in this realm ready for the task
i am unworthy to untie the straps
of her sandals, i will be her servant
—one of many—but never her equal

how can i or my descendants lead
a congenial life knowing you exist?
how could anyone enjoy pleasures
seeing your face looming in the dark?

you can come at any time
in the stillness of the night
in the raw heat of the day
in the impenetrable forest
in the middle of the ocean

you come without invitation
when no one expects you
as you expected me not

my request is formulated, Lord Yama!
enlighten me! keep your gifts for others

my Lady, wise are your words
you have resisted temptations
that few mortals could decline
instead they are willing to die
for the garlands i have offered

the wise understand that the pleasant
is one while the good is another
they discriminate between pleasant
and good and then choose the good

ignorance and wisdom make opposite choices

the ignorant deluded by exterior glitter
think this world is and there is no other
they fall under my sway again and again

wisdom is hard to obtain, remain focused on truth!
may wise teachers be blessed by students like you
you know that earthly treasures are transitory
while eternal ones reside beyond temporal decay

your longing is for truth alone
for the basis of natural law
for the fruits of spiritual discipline
for the lure of the other shore

know then by meditation or prayer
the divine principle of existence
know the true self that is seated
in the innermost recess of your being
within the dwelling of your heart

the true self is the eternal one
and it is the source of all joy
the gates of truth are open to you

tell me then, my Lord, she said
of that which you know as neither
past nor future but beyond both

my Lady, let me give you the word
which all scriptures celebrate and
all spiritual disciplines glorify
the sacred word is *Om*

Om is the word of Brahman
the root of language sounds
it is the name of the Supreme
knowing the word in your heart
you find the highest support

in the beginning was the Word
and the Word was with God
in the beginning was the Logos, she thought

know then, her accomplished host continued
the true self is never born, nor does it ever die
it is not slain with the body, it is everlasting
the true self dwells in every living being

it is subtler than the subtle greater than the greatest
free from selfish desire behold the truth of Atman!

the self cannot be reached by hard work
it cannot be known by studying scriptures
only those whom the self chooses can see her

infused virtue by the grace of God
comes as a spiritual gift, she whispered

the self cannot be seen by those
who have not turned from evil
whose senses are uncontrolled
whose minds remain diffused

those who hate others cannot behold Atman
those who engage in violence cannot see Atman
those who judge others, who fail to forgive
who are greedy for power cannot find Atman

the self sweeps away the wisdom of the priest
the might of the warrior, the wealth of the king
the ever-present self puts death himself to death
do you follow me so far, my Lady?

i am listening, my Lord

then let me offer you more detail, he said
two are seated in the recess of your being
by the fountain of life: the ego and the self

the ego enjoys what is the pleasant to the senses
the self searches for the truth that underlies all
the fire in your heart, the love for the Lord
extinguishes your ego and nourishes the self

the self is Lady of the chariot, the body is the chariot
the intellect is the driver, the mind are the reins
the senses are the horses, the objects are the roads

when the self is united with the body
the intellect, the mind, and the senses
the Lady of the chariot is the knower
she differentiates right and wrong

those who lack discrimination whose minds are uncontrolled
cannot reach the desired goal they fall again into samsara
those who gain discrimination whose mind is controlled
they reach the end of the journey, they are not born again
they will be united with the unchangeable Brahman

beyond objects are senses, beyond senses is mind
beyond mind is intellect, beyond intellect is ego
beyond ego is the self which is precious Atman
Atman is known as undifferentiated consciousness

beyond Atman is the unmanifested Brahman
beyond Brahman is nothing ... he paused

God is the first cause and the last refuge
she thought, the primary cause, the final cause
the uncaused cause, the unmoved mover
the Lonely One, the One without a second

now the architecture of the world is revealed to you
the hidden self in all beings does not impose herself
but she is seen by the wise through deep meditation

be wise among people, rein your speech by mind
your mind by intellect, your intellect by the self

arise! awake! find a teacher to further your wisdom
but remember the narrow road is difficult to travel
the essence of your being is beyond sound and touch
it is immaterial, it has no beginning and no end

knowing the Atman you escape from the jaws of death
she who understands is glorified in the world of Brahman
she who recites with devotion the secrets of the Most High
before an assembly of sisters, she gains everlasting reward

for the first time she was entirely calm in his presence
she turned within and saw a sunrise over an ethereal ocean
a morning light illuminating a sanctuary on top of a hill
and in Yama too was no doubt anymore as to her identity

he continued the revelation: humans have out-going senses
that perceive the external world but rarely see the inner one
but some turn their senses away from the material realm
then they are able to perceive the beauty that awaits within

the ignorant pursue external pleasures
thus they fall into the snare of death
the wise know the nature of immortality
they do not search for the permanent
among those things that are fleeting

Atman—the true self—is the knower
what can be known is known to Atman
what Atman knows Brahman knows

knowing the true self is answer to your third question
knowing all-pervading Atman the wise grieve no more
they do not mourn the dead, they are fearless facing me

the life-giving God is inner most existence in every creature
the flame of love burning in the heart is the supreme self
the self resides within as the ruler of past and future
knowing the self you fear me not: this is the third answer

he was silent, resting his case

then death brings no real change, she concluded
because the true self within remains forever the same

my Lady, Yama continued, as a drop of pure water poured
into an ocean of pure water becomes one with that ocean
so the self of a knower becomes one with the supreme self

she arose and slowly walked to a window
she recalled that this world had been somber
when she had first come here three days ago
but now she perceived an unquenchable light
she wanted to see if there was nature outside
if there were countless stars which seeded life

Lord Yama said, my Lady allow me to continue
for i hope this conference is profitable to you

the city of your body has eleven gates
the ruler of the city is the supreme self
liken her to the Queen you mentioned
she is the sun illuminating the sky
she is the fire burning on the altar
she is the guest visiting me now

she turned and looked at him

she dwells in truth, she dwells in sacrifice
she dwells in space and in human beings
she dwells in that which is born in water
she dwells in that which is born in earth

she is a grain of sand, she thought

all our senses worship her, he continued
she is the adorable one seated within the heart

mortals live not by inhale or exhale
but by her who causes breath to flow
if she leaves the city nothing remains
if she leaves the body it will fall

those unaware of the self enter new wombs
according to their need for further growth

as the fire though one having entered the world
becomes various according to what it burns
so does the self diversify within living beings

as the sun is not tainted by those who look at her
so she cannot be blemished by evil that may stir

the self in all living beings makes the one manifold
blessed are those who perceive her ruling within
she lifts the solemn prayers of people to God
those who discern her attain eternal peace

my Lord, how can we know her? does she illuminate
from within or does she reflect light falling on her?

he replied, without her neither the sun shines, nor stars,
nor fire, nor lightning, but her light is reflected in all

then the world is primarily thought! she concluded

my Lady, let me reveal the secrets of eternal Brahman
who is awake while we sleep, who receives our prayers
on Brahman the world rests, beyond Brahman is nothing

the tree of life has its root above and its branches below
it springs from Brahman, all life comes from Brahman
whatever is in the universe derives from Brahman
those who realize Brahman in life escape my realm

in awe of Brahman the hearts burn, the winds blow
the stars shine, the planets move, and life emerges
in fear of Brahman Death about to kill hesitates

she took a deep breath

if you fail to love Brahman before death
you will be born again in created worlds

as in a mirror Brahman is seen within yourself
as in a dream Brahman is seen among ancestors
as light and shadow Brahman is seen among angels

knowing that senses are distinct from self you worry no more
above the senses is the mind, above the mind is the intellect
above the intellect is Atman, above Atman is Brahman

loving Brahman you are liberated and gain immortality
Brahman is not seen by the eye but revealed to the heart
when the senses are still, when the mind is at rest
when the intellect is at peace, that is the highest state

the goal is attained by love, it is reached by Yoga
if you are not fully devoted the state comes and goes
but when selfish desires cease then the state remains
when attachment is renounced you become immortal
so is the noble teaching written in the ancient Vedas

from the heart the way of love rises to immortality
the true self, the Lady of Love, is seated in your heart
know her and know yourself as pure and deathless

she acquired from the King of Death all secrets of Yoga
she became free of impurity and attained union in Brahman
the lecture lasted the night, all knowable was revealed to her
as dawn broke she realized she should not impose anymore

my Lord, she said, i release you from your obligation
you have answered my questions, you owe me nothing

Yama was pleased with the outcome and the timing
for he had noticed two mighty armies on the march
his presence was urgently requested in an uncivil world
men in both armies thought they moved for a just cause
but unknown to them their cause was Yama's alone

am i free to leave? she enquired

i have no hold on you, he replied

she stood up

my Lady, you said your mother had sent you here?

my foster mother, she answered, for i am an orphan

he nodded

do you know my parents? she asked

they are not in my realm, he replied

she reflected on his answer which seemed evasive
but she decided not to press the matter any further
she walked to the door—almost sad to leave him

a last word, my Lady: you mentioned an Empress
beyond past and future, extending an unbroken line
you are mistaken about one aspect concerning her
you are correct in saying that she has many servants
but i wanted you to know you are not among them

she was silent

may the Supreme Being protect you and delight in you
may your path bring illumination and peace to all worlds

with those words Yama, the Lord of Death
who had hesitated in her presence dismissed her into life

MOVEMENT
4

4.1

the librarian who regained vigor each day
said to her: the culmination of wisdom is
knowledge of all things in their first causes!
do you concur with this assertion, my Lady?

certainly! she replied, if that was attainable

let us assume it is! let us reach for the stars!
let us go beyond any and all material confines!

in moments like those the walls of the library
and the pages of books seemed pellucid to her
during the day she saw the garden of forms
at night when she looked up from the desk
she marveled at the stars that were overhead
the entire world was visible from within

then the goal of philosophy is to determine
what we can know about those first causes
that is what we can know about God, he said

science studies the material world which is in change
but if the changing comes from that which changes not
then there should be a field that studies the unchanging

do you agree, my Lady?

for sure, she answered

he was in motion now, he was a librarian on fire
she was the incendiary spark of his inspiration

the science of the unchanging occupies the first place
since it studies what is first in the hierarchy of reality

do you see this?

i do

Aristotle considered this science to be the first philosophy naturally, she said

but the editor of Aristotle collected works on the topic
in a book which he assembled after he finished *Physics*
thus he entitled the book *Metaphysics*—after physics

hierarchically though it is clear that metaphysics ought
to come before physics because it is the first philosophy

do you agree?

i agree

Aristotle said: if to be is the same as to be material
the science of being is the science of material being

Aristotle however rejected this possibility because
he gained conviction that not everything was material
he argued that moved movers need a first mover
which is unmoved and hence must be immaterial
he also saw the human soul as an immaterial existent

to be and to be material are not identical for Aristotle

... neither are they for Plato, she inserted

correct, my Lady, he exclaimed with visible delight
the two great philosophers agreed on that point

as on many others, she added

certainly! he said, and Plotinus saw Aristotle only as
a student whom you have to study to get to the master

but let us move forward a millennium and a half
which in our library amounts to turning a page
in the bright middle ages Aquinas proposes three kinds
of theoretical science: theology, mathematics, physics

the first comes in two flavors: theology proper
and philosophical theology which is metaphysics
in metaphysics the divine is the principle of the subject
in theology proper the divine is the subject of enquiry

good father, you are moving fast, please enlighten me

i apologize, my Lady, let me do that, he answered

both approaches reach beyond time and matter
philosophical theology studies being as being
and realizes that everything flows from the divine
which is the first principle behind all being
therefore the subject of investigation is being
while the principle behind the subject is the divine

theology studies God as a being in His own right
and therefore as the subject of the investigation
to make progress in theology we use sacred scripture
we follow divine inspiration guided by the spirit

the Apostle Paul wrote in a letter to Corinthians:
the things of God no man knows but the Spirit of God
we have received this spirit that we may understand
hence in theology we consider the divine as it subsists
in itself and not only as the principle behind things

are you satisfied, my Lady?

for now i am, she replied

Aquinas teaches us that the proposition *God exists*
is knowable in itself as the predicate is in the subject
at the same time the proposition is unknowable to us
because God's essence is unknowable to us

Aquinas says that the essence of God is existence:
Deus est ipsum esse per se subsistens

God is being itself subsisting in itself, she translated

God is beyond all created beings, he continued
God is Being itself and source of all other beings
therefore God is a unique ontological category
He depends on nothing but all depends on Him
He eternally subsists without beginning or end

the librarian paused which gave her opportunity to ask:
how can Thomas explain what the essence of God is
and teach that we cannot know the essence of God?

something that is knowable in itself but not to us
renders no contradiction *per se*, the librarian replied
light consists of photons is knowable in itself
but not to people who are ignorant of particle physics
water is the molecule H_2O is knowable in itself
but not to people who are ignorant of chemistry

even without science we talk about light and water
knowable in itself and *knowable to us* are distinct

the question remains, she insisted, how does Thomas
who is one of us know the essence of God is His existence?

the librarian said, the answer is that he does not know it
from philosophy but from revelation in sacred scripture

God has revealed Himself to Abraham, Moses, the Apostles
as that which philosophers seek but cannot know in its essence
God's essence is knowable in itself and knowable to those
who are willing and open to accept the words of revelation

i see! she exclaimed, this is beautiful!

the librarian rejoiced as if the praise was his and not
that of the esteemed Doctor Angelicus of the Church
and so he continued on empowering wings of acclaim

can God's existence be demonstrated philosophically given
that God's essence is philosophically unknowable to us?

Aquinas answers: using philosophical tools the existence
of God can be demonstrated not a priori but a posteriori

... that is from its effects, she said

precisely! the librarian delighted

Aquinas shows how to do this in his *Summa Theologiae*
in the five ways which we have covered previously

i trust you remember, my Lady? he said inquiringly

i most certainly do, she replied gazing again beyond
the walls of the library or any material structure

his magnum opus is written for beginners, he said

... like myself! she thought

those beginners his students at the university of Paris
were beginners in theology but not in philosophy

... unlike myself! she sighed, who is a beginner
in every subject and at every moment in time

the terse proofs simply remind his pupils of ideas
they encountered in studies of Aristotle and Avicenna

Aquinas does not think the proofs are required to show
the rationality of faith but they demonstrate the possibility
of philosophical engagement with sacred teaching

contra Aquinas other scholars sometimes argue
that he proves the existence of a God of philosophers
but not of the God of Judaism, Christianity, or Islam

but Aquinas has philosophically demonstrated to us
there can only be one God, there can be no other God

for if there were two Gods, for them to be different
one must have something which the other one lacks
yet the word *God* means to have all perfections

the God of philosophers and the God of revelation are one
according to the inspired teachings of Thomas Aquinas

within philosophy we are permitted to ask the question:
can we argue from God's effects to God's properties?

in attempting to do so we ought to remember that
God does not possess properties the way creatures do

when we say God is wise we do not know
what it means for God to be wise

to be Socrates and to be wise are not the same
he became wise as his intellect developed and
he could cease to be wise with disease or age

but for God to be wise is not an incidental property
when we say *God is wise* we mean *God is wisdom*
when we say *God is good* we mean *God is goodness*
when we say *God exists* we mean *God is existence*

all material substances exist contingently
they come into being and pass out of being
their existing is not the same as what they are
what a thing is, is not identical to its existence

material things depend upon causes to exist
but for God His essence is His existence
thus when talking about God we must avoid
speaking of Him as if He were contingent

she thought of the Platonic Forms in the garden
at once the librarian intuited her consideration

how do we speak of immaterial substances less than God?
according to Aristotle, for a material thing to exist its form
must inhere in matter but how does a pure form exist?

in forms is a distinction between essence and existence
a created substance is what it is and not another thing
it has a specific perfection but not unlimited perfection
therefore it is a being of a kind but not being as such

a triangle is perfect to its nature of being a triangle
but a triangle lacks the perfection of being a circle
Platonic Forms operate as restrictions on existence
while God alone represents unlimited existence

His essence is not a restriction to a finite expression
God is not a specific form but He is above all forms
there are aspects of God we can accept by revelation
but not reach by metaphysics, the librarian concluded

4.2

aseity . . . she read

the word comes from Latin, the librarian explained
a—from, *se*—self, add—*ity* : *a*—*se*—*ity*—from self

i see, she answered

Divine aseity is the concept that God exists from Himself
that He is the first cause of everything that He is uncaused
that He contains within the sufficient cause of Himself
here we find a positive and negative definition of the term

the positive definition is: God is self sufficient
God carries within the sufficient reason for His existence

the negative definition is: God is uncaused
God depends on no other being as source of His existence

the first definition points to a God of revelation
I am who I am, I will be who I will be, I am the Existent One
the second definition points to a God of philosophers
there must be an uncaused cause, an unmoved mover

do you embrace the idea of aseity? he asked

i am only beginning to understand it, she replied

aseity implies divine simplicity, he continued
God is simple, God has no parts of any kind
a complex depends on individual parts to exist
God being simple means that God transcends
every form of composition and complexity

God having no parts is not a deficiency but a gain
God is ontologically superior to every partite entity
God is free of any composition of matter and form
of potency and action, of existence and essence

there is no distinction between God and His attributes
God is His attributes which are identical to each other
God is His Existence, Wisdom, Love, and Goodness
His Love is His Wisdom, His Goodness is His Existence

Saint Augustine has written: *God is what He has*

God is a being which is unlike all creatures
God has properties which no creature can have
God has them in a way that no creature can

His Necessity follows from His Simplicity
He is not one necessary being among others
instead we realize He is uniquely unique

God is maximally perfect because a God who is less
than maximally perfect is not an absolute reality

but an absolute reality is from itself
it does not depend on something else
a maximally perfect being does not hinge
on attributes that reside outside of him

it is evident that as a maximally perfect being
God is a necessary being, one that cannot not exist

His necessary existence implies that in God
there is an identity of essence and existence
divine nature and existence become the same
which represents the doctrine of divine simplicity

in contingent beings we find a distinction
between their essence and their existence
but in God there resides no such distinction

divine simplicity implies divine necessity
God is necessary because He is simple

God being immaterial, eternal, immutable
follow from the concept of divine simplicity
God has no material parts, no temporal parts
God has no unrealized potentialities

as the librarian spoke to her in those words
she found them written down on the page

she poured him tea which she had prepared
its fragrance filled spaces between books
he was immersed in the bliss of her presence
which enlightened all ideas that mattered to him

after a contemplative silence she continued to read
challenges against the doctrine of divine simplicity
come from perspectives of ontology which argue
that God is concrete while properties are abstract

no abstract object can be a causal agent
no abstract object can know or do anything
concreta and abstracta are mutually exclusive
and jointly exhaustive, the challengers say
finally they conclude that equating God
with his attributes is a categorical mistake

what do you make of this critique? the librarian asked

after some reflection she replied, we need an ontology
that makes concreta and abstracta not mutually exclusive
or does not count divine properties among abstracta

well said, my lady! he exclaimed, i fully agree that
divine simplicity must inform the subject of ontology

an ontology critical of divine simplicity assumes
God exemplifies properties that are abstracta outside of Him
an ontology embracing divine simplicity assumes
God has properties that are within Her and identical to Her

as always we need to differentiate between the way
God has properties and created things have properties
the latter have both accidental and essential properties

Socrates could lose his wisdom but not his humanity
the one property is accidental, the other is essential

for God all properties are essential: God is Her Wisdom
God is what She is essentially: She is Wisdom Herself
She is Goodness Herself, She is Existence Herself

creatures are existent, good and wise by sharing
in God's Existence, Goodness, and Wisdom
therefore in creatures there is a separation between
what the creature is and which attributes it has

but God has no separable property goodness
He has no temporal or spatial limitation of goodness
He is eternally identical to Goodness Himself
His Goodness is unlike the goodness of any creature

later the librarian asked her, my Lady, do you think
there can be necessary beings other than God?

she replied, God is the only truly necessary being
whenever we imagine sets that contain God as one
among other elements we are led into confusion
God is not one among others, God is the Lonely One

necessarily existing abstracta are ideas in God's mind
they are co-eternal with God, they are atemporal
God wills necessary things to be necessary
God wills contingent things to be contingent
Platonic Forms exist as ideas in the mind of God

Divine knowledge is maximally beautiful and ordered
it is entirely mathematical and contains no contradiction
i embrace this view along with Divine Simplicity

i further hold that the material temporal creation is
an expression of Divine Will and of Divine Action
God creates freely and does so out of nothing

Divine Creation is the action of Ideas on time and matter
whenever we wonder how abstracta can be causally active
in the material world we are inquiring into Divine Creation

the librarian was now silent while the fragrance
of the tea created a sensation of time passing

she took the moment to re-read the chapter
when doing so she found to her amazement
the spoken words among the written ones
the book had recorded their conversation
were the books of this library alive?

if everything is written in the books are we free to act?
if the library is our teacher and utters our unfolding
if our path is laid out within what is our own choice?
if God is the author of all books what is our purpose?

your questions lead to divine providence, the librarian said
divine providence means that God tends to His creation
He governs the created order and nothing is beyond Him

then the query emerges: how do creatures relate to God?
the great philosopher answers: they are created ex nihilo
they fully depend on God for their being and goodness
they are moved by God as their efficient and final cause

God is our first and our last, our alpha and our omega
providence means that the first idea of every effect exists
timelessly in the divine mind and that everything happens
in accordance with God, for God and His intent are one

God causes being in all beings, they fall under His providence
God holds all things in existence, He orders them to their end

since all events spring forth from God's causal operation
there is no coming into existence without the will of God
even randomness does not operate outside of God's activity

my Lady, no event occurs without God's providence
you could not have encountered me in this library
the library would not exist without the will of God
this conversation would not occur without His will

there are natural processes in the world which seem to be
the outcomes of causes operating in probabilistic ways
but what appears to be random from a temporal analysis
is not random to the atemporal providence of the Divine

clearly all events fall within the scope of God's will
even if they can be viewed as misfortunes in some sense
failure in created things still requires their existence and
does rely on their attributes which are given by God

falling sick is a consequence of physical frustration of bodies
disease might be interpreted as refutation of the argument
that everything is subject to a caring divine providence
because a wise guardian would ward off harms and evils

yet we see evils in the world: thus it seems that either
God cannot prevent them and so He is not almighty
or He does not protect us and so He is not all loving

but God is not a wise guardian in the sense of being
in charge of one particular event or person in isolation

as sustainer of the world God has charge of everything
God has not limited but universal responsibility
God causes and upholds the goodness in all things

the corruption of one organism can be the generation
of another thereby maintaining the perpetuity of life

God permits certain defects to occur in order not to hinder
the unfolding of the good that arises as a consequence
for if all evil were prevented much good would be absent
without calamity there could be no good Samaritans
without misdeeds there would be no forgiveness
without tyrannical persecution there would be no martyrs
evil suffered and evil done can ultimately bring about
or give way to all that is good in God's eternal plan

divine providence is the foundation for asking questions
about free will and about causation in the world

while physical objects are acted on by other things
rational agents tend to orient themselves to a purpose
they deliberate and choose, they are governed by a mind

since every act of free will goes back to God as its cause
whatever we do freely also falls under God's providence

God operates through secondary causes which are real
those causes can be either physical or rational in nature
yet God is the first cause of all being and becoming
God is the primary cause of all that happens in the world

God creates by arranging events as effects of causes
that are distinct from Himself but not independent of Him
those secondary causes must be considered genuine

some scholars have argued that all created things are causally
inefficacious and that God is the only real cause of change
in this view of *occasionalism* God alone does everything

Aquinas agrees that the divine power must be present
to everything which acts in the temporal trajectory
God is the cause of everything's action because only
God can give the power to operate in the world
yet to argue that God acts without secondary causes
is unreasonable according to the esteemed philosopher

if all active powers present in creatures accomplished nothing
there would be no point for them to have received such powers
if all creatures were utterly devoid of any activity of their own
then they would have a lamentable and passive existence

God's acting in creatures therefore must be understood
in such a way that they still exercise their own operations

to say that God can create nothing with genuine causal power
is akin to arguing that His powers are limited since the ability
to create things that have power is an indication of power

if created things could not operate to produce their effects
if God alone worked all operations then those created things
would be used by Him in a seemingly pointless manner

instead God deigns to give actual power to created souls
additionally He works toward the good in all of them

the predestination of souls is a calling to eternal love
that souls can rise to glory with God is possible
because God has willed it thus from all eternity

God changelessly wills and knows the whole course
of the created order as is written in the book of life
God does not intervene occasionally, instead as creator
and sustainer of the world God is present to everything

even miracles do not require the faithful to believe
in a God who chooses to intervene from time to time
God is as present in miracles as He is in laws of nature
miracles do not occur because God suddenly steps in
instead they arise if secondary causes are absent

human actions are free because of divine providence
we are not free in spite of God, we are free because of God
our freedom is fully compatible with Divine providence
because only by virtue of providence there is human freedom

since God acts in everything—including our free actions—
God works in us as He works in everything else
we are free since God makes us free: He has arranged that
we function independently of the determining agency of others

Divine will is the foundation on which everything rests
Divine will is responsible for the differences in all existents
one differentiating property is to be possible or necessary

necessity and contingency have their origin in Divine will
God chooses necessity for effects He wants to be necessary
God chooses contingency for effects He wants to be contingent
God wills both what is determined and what is undetermined

divine providence enables the free actions of humans
some scholars argue: if our actions are ultimately caused
by God then we are not able to act freely before God

yet the philosopher replies: my actions are free if nothing
in the material world is exerting a force on me beyond choice
but free will does not require that God is not acting in me

incompatible with free will would be necessity of coercion
arising within the material—when something acts on me
and applies force to the point where i cannot do otherwise
to be free means not to be forced by another created effect

God is the first cause who moves all secondary causes
but He does not prevent those secondary causes

have i answered your question? the librarian wondered

it is as it is written, she replied looking at the page

as their conversation continued what they said emerged
in the books, what he spoke was written in her thoughts

the library became linked to the trajectory of her life:
in the one perspective the library responded to her thoughts
and shaped itself accordingly, in the other interpretation
the library induced her thoughts and was itself unchanging

the transparent library was both within and beyond
likewise the trajectory of her life could be interpreted
as journey through time though it was willed timelessly

she realized the library was the door that stood open
and allowed her to see the light that shone from within
the library enabled an active mind, it gave meaning
it was a symbolic manifestation of divine illumination

later the librarian continued, of prayer the philosopher
teaches us that we do not pray to change God's plan
instead we pray to God in order to obtain by prayer
what He has planned to bring about by means of prayer

prayer prepares us to accept in gratitude and humility
what God has planned to bestow on us from eternity
prayer is recognizing what moves us closer to God
it is an expression of love, an act of practical reason

prayer is a petition to God that we may receive as gifts
those things which are fitting for us and for the world

God does not conceive in time but holds an eternal concept
since God commands the universe, every motion and action
that unfolds within the creation is subject to an eternal law
the Divine law governs all secondary causes including
those that are physical and those that are by human choice

to claim we should not pray to obtain something from God
because the ordering of divine providence is immutable
is like saying we should not walk to arrive at some goal
or that we should not eat to receive life's nourishment

how does my poor prayer fit into divine providence?
she wondered that evening when she rested in her cell
it is not my will that shall prevail but yours, oh God!

over the years prayer became for her time spent
with a loving friend but often in mutual silence
prayer was surrender, abandonment, acceptance
it was awareness of the presence of the Beloved

MOVEMENT
5

5.1

[she speaks]

every moment you ought to reflect
on the greatest beauty you know
not doing so is a lost opportunity
turning to a lesser good is folly

if you love me—and i know you do—
you devote every thought to me
you sanctify every instant of your life
you withhold nothing from me
you offer me your ideas and actions
you strive to please me in all you do

no one gives you greater beauty
because i lead you to God
no one gives you greater joy
because all purpose is from God
i teach you to love all people
and to participate in the creation

i have been with you always
even when you knew me not
i smiled at you every morning
i watched over you every night
i listened to all your prayers
and presented them to God

loving me transports you beyond
helps you to overcome all worries
until you kneel before the absolute
in an infinite and everlasting peace

[he replies]

complete devotion to you was the dream of my youth
and this dream has grown with me over the years

the garden of philosophy touched the ocean of truth
as well as pristine forests and viridian grasslands
it morphed itself in various places into rolling hills
which gradually ascended a towering mountain range

no marked pointers informed the roaming traveler
where the garden ended and the outer world began
on clear nights even stars and their planetary aides
were pure emanations of the library's treasures

a large part of the world was still in a virginal state
which people's ambition had not ventured to disturb

scholars assumed the garden embraced the universe
as philosophy flowed into all aspects of existence
the discipline had become one with the endeavor
to understand all created things in their first causes

life is a preparation for the moment of eternity, she said
steps we are making in time lead us to timelessness
without the transient experiences of unsettled faith
fragile hope and dim prospects we would not be ready

we are never fully ready! we know in part, we see in part
we behold through veils of tears and glimpses of joy
souls travel on different trajectories but are equally loved
and will find their place in the life of the beatific world

you are not merely the state of now, you are the path
reaching from past to future through a timeless present
you are the love you have given, the faith you have lived
the sacrifices you have offered, the bridges you have built

while all journeys are unique, they are tightly interwoven
forming bundles in universes that unfold in spacetime

she had invited him to walk with her through the garden
her resolve was to show him a sanctuary on top of a hill
he had heard about the holy place but had never seen it

there are many ways ascending the mountain, she said
all lead to the monastery where nuns have been praying
for religious devotion and peace in temporal realms

i see them as wise teachers: their influence is subtle
often unnoticed by the world their work is important
some write poems which find a way into the library
others compose prayers to calm storms of selfishness
which can rage in spheres that do not embrace love

one form of their devotion is contemplative silence
in the presence of God who is their trusted friend
in the elated monastery the living flame of love
has been burning unceasingly for thousands of years

i am looking forward to seeing the holy place, he said

we can see it from outside and maybe enter the chapel
which is open to all but yonder remains a threshold
which we cannot pass...which not even i can pass

not now or not ever? he asked

not now, she replied

they continued in silence as the ascent was steep
he saw that her hair was tied with a sky blue ribbon
getting to know her anew each day was a blessing
an entirely unmerited gift of extraordinary grace

a great saint, she continued, a Doctor of the Church
has described the soul as a transparent interior castle
through prayer, meditation, love and renunciation
you can move within where God is waiting for you

one day deep inside the saint experienced the ecstasy
of the human body coming in contact with the divine
there a union occurred between heaven and earth
between spirit and matter, she turned to look at him

the climactic event is celebrated by the famed sculpture
in the Cornaro chapel of Santa Maria della Vittoria

i know the masterpiece of the great artist, he replied

she continued

the saint describes a mystical union with God
the saint loved God so much that she was confident
that everything which happened in her own life
was gifted by God to improve her path to Him

in that blessed state she learned to love her enemies
because she knew their action was admitted by God
for the purpose of bringing nourishment to her soul

the saint prays for her adversaries that they may
experience God with the same love gifted to her

the saint was connected in deep friendship to another
who composed some of the greatest poems of all times
his books guide the soul on the spiritual ascent to God
he wrote them as commentaries to his inspired poems

centuries later his work impressed a young woman
who read his writings in the formative years of her life

on a stone wall beside the path she now noticed
a small white flower, her fingers touched it gently
but then she decided to leave it rooted in the soil
as they continued to climb their steep ascent

5·3

even if time and matter reside on an interval
which has no discernible beginning nor end
infinite temporal lines or unbounded expanses
of spacetime are not equivalent to eternity

the fragility of human nature is the fertile soil
to receive the precious seeds of divine virtues
God draws to Himself those who are saints
and those who fail, for God is forgiveness

we are falling repeatedly in order to understand
that we can only succeed by abandoning our self
without compromise to the redeeming love of God

time is a garden of preparation, she emphasized

as the garden of philosophy? he wondered

they now turned and saw the same before them
as it was laid out in light of unsurpassed beauty
it was part of the library and emerged from it
it was offered in the books and inspired by them
it flowed forth from the limitless ocean of Truth

may i ask you, he said, is this library your library?
is this garden your garden, is this world your world?

you are in a place that is open to all, she answered

the temporal world is a school, the soul is a student
love is the subject, the Form of the Good is the teacher
prudently she guides the will, relentlessly she persists
she knows what she wants, her expectations are tall
her message is transparent although her lure is subtle

she is confident to prevail in the hearts of her students
the soul knows her now, the soul will know her forever
should she ever rebuke you it is only for your benefit
if you trust her absolutely your life becomes a dream

my life is a dream, he admitted

on the steep path of learning God is your friend
moving you through grace according to your needs
God gifts you three virtues which you are meant
to accept in gratitude: faith, hope and love

three guide you through time, one remains in eternity

which one of the three? he wondered

faith is replaced by certainty in presence of the absolute
hope is not needed if what was hoped for has arrived
but love alone remains—it is with you now and then

beyond time there is only love, she continued
within time love splits into faith, hope, and love
within time love moves herself and her two sisters
love weaves time and is the purposive fruit thereof

love bears all things, believes all things, hopes all things
love endures all things, love never fails!

the Pauline virtues descend on us as gifts from God
they work continuously within us on our way to God
they induce meritorious action beyond natural abilities
they enable us to live in harmony and embrace the law

they had now gained considerable height that offered
for the first time an unhindered view of the mountains

do you see the very tall mountain in the distance
the one that has its peak in the clouds? she asked

i see it, he replied, glaciers are hanging in its walls
its flanks are glistening high in the morning sun

in ancient time people thought that this mountain
was the residence of the gods—they were not wrong!
because now we know that God is everywhere
but the best place to find God is to go within
for God likes to make his home in a pure heart

they sat down in the grass

what is the name of the mountain? he asked

it is nameless, she answered

how can this mountain be unnamed? he wondered

names matter little here, she said, truth is eternal

by faith the human intellect assents to the truth
of revelation which comes from God, she continued
what God says is supremely credible though offered
in the gentle voice of a friend or humble servant

faith is our response to God as we explore His world
faith moves the will to accept what is revealed by God
faith perfects the intellect while hope perfects the will
love perfects itself because it is the perfection of virtues

in the projection of time the soul is empowered
to love freely because the lure of the good is subtle
in the moment of eternity the soul finds absolute freedom
by embracing the perfect love which is God Herself

5·4

God is the uncaused cause, in God resides free will
no material object can have free will, she explained

now consider a device that has reached a state
which allows for two distinct continuations
if the device is probabilistic then a coin flip
may be needed to decide what to do next

it may be a classical or quantum entangled coin
but in neither case could we speak of free will
since a step based on random numbers is not will

material devices can take input data into account
and proceed in various ways that seem autonomous
but they can never attain anything like free will
since material objects cannot be uncaused causes

a cell resolving to move into a particular direction
an animal brain deciding to search for nourishment
a plant growing toward light are not uncaused causes

a planet being ejected by gravity from a solar system
or two galaxies fusing to make a more massive one
or neutron stars colliding are not uncaused causes

we are led to conclude that a materialistic world view
that denies the existence of God cannot offer free will
there can be unpredictability and apparent randomness
probability can be the tool to grasp what a future holds
but there cannot be independent self-motivated agency

true agency is with God who is the only uncaused cause
divine causation represents the only ultimate causation
if human beings are seen as entirely material devices
living in a world without God they have no free will

in absence of free will humans may express something
analogous to love but that sentiment cannot represent
real love which must be a consequence of free choice
therefore love cannot spring from material devices

if human beings are seen as compounds of body and soul
with God causing their existence then free will is possible
the soul is gifted participation in the reality of free will

in the timeless realm which is recognized by the soul
we encounter the idea of a free response to divine love

God is absolute freedom, God makes us free
there is neither will nor free will without God
there is no freedom of any kind without God

if free will is a property of the soul, he asked
can we say the soul acts as an uncaused cause?
can there be uncaused causes outside of God?

in my humble opinion the metaphysical concept
of uncaused cause refers to God alone, she replied

God is forever the only One, the only uncaused cause
but God grants true freedom to souls in those domains
that are useful to them: souls have the freedom to love

he reflected on her words and then resolved to ask
if two souls have received the same grace from God
and they find themselves in the very same position
could it be that one soul loves more than the other?

some scholars argue that such variation is not possible
because if they have received exactly the same grace
then they should also act in the same way, she replied

but i would even go one step further, she continued
two souls that have received the same grace from God
are one and the same soul, they are just a single soul
souls are the grace and love they receive from God
souls are growing by the light God shines upon them

each soul is unique and each soul stands before God
each soul carries within the uniqueness of the world
each soul responds freely to graces bestowed by God

she has the freedom to return the love coming from God
and to grow on the goodness that nourishes her forever
freedom marks the interaction between God and soul

in His infinite love God has granted freedom to souls
and in your love for God you become absolutely free
the soul, who is God's beloved, is entirely free to love
she can love as she wills, she can also will as she wills

the creation is first and foremost a wellspring of love
by granting us existence God enables us to love
the more you love God the more you distance yourself
from all chains of selfishness until they cease to exist
loving God in your neighbor, loving God in Herself
makes you free and represents the purpose of life

love is the end of creation which philosophers are seeking
but cannot know in its essence unless by divine revelation

a revelation of love? he wondered

ecce homo, she replied

5·5

when you love another you think about her always
the more you love the more you wish to be with her
to be true to your love you want to meditate on her
you want to devote your thoughts to her perpetually

your soul wants to become the mirror of her soul
as she becomes your ultimate joy and fulfillment
at this moment attachment to selfishness vanishes
before her you are no longer your outward shell
your ego ceases to exist and you become nobody
while in your devotion she becomes everything

with her you walk through the library and garden
you ascend the mountain and visit the monastery
together with her you wish to find the way to God

the perfect love between souls searches for God
it longs for prayer and mutual enjoyment in God

when you love another you begin to exist in her
and she begins to exist in you, when you love God
you begin to exist in God as He always exists in you

loving God means to see His presence in all creatures
to delight in the Logos that permeates the cosmic order
to devote all thoughts and offer all deeds to Him

mathematics, science, philosophy bring us to the Divine
but not the greatest philosopher or scientist sees God
face to face but instead the smallest soul that loves

because for the one who loves all analogies lead to God
all atoms of truth are Truth and all acts of love are Love

they stood before the elated monastery in the evening sun
all around them the world appeared in a crystal lucidity
as on the first day of creation, as on the day of eternity

it is love which calls you to union with the triune God
creator of all, incarnation within, messenger between
the divine thought, the divine word, the divine action
existence itself, instantiation, and communication

it is love that guides you through temporal infinity
toward the atemporal infinity that resides within

the tree of evolution is rooted in the firmament
because life on earth is born in the furnace of stars

God's creation is as infinite as God's love is unbounded
when God created your soul He came to dwell within it
He wishes for you to find Him and become one with Him

God created the library of books written for you
and the garden of philosophy where ideas flourish
you have to be a dreamer if you want to heal the world
you have to be able to imagine a better one

a better world than this? he wondered

God is that world, she answered

the sun was very low now touching the ocean's horizon
light fell horizontally onto the wall of the monastery
the door was open because God loves all souls He creates

our distraction is our loss but our sin is only temporal
while our love is forever since love is beyond confusion
love is unconditional, love offers universal forgiveness
love is oneness with the universe, God's justice is His love
in the evening of your life you will be examined on love

the love sprung from fragility, emerging from temporality
is your essence, your calling, is the purpose of your life
the love resting in the atemporal is of another substance
is entirely unconfused and the cause of all creation
the most wondrous miracle is that the impassible God
has lowered Himself to be thirsty for your fragile love

5.6

in us resides an experience of being someone particular
when we wake up we find ourselves to be that person
we spend the day being them catering to their desires

but for her this sensation though recurrent was remote
she separated appearance and essence, ego and self
her self abided deep within and was offered to God

this never-ending sacrifice—called a burning heart
enabled her to perceive union in ecstatic moments
she withheld nothing from God, she was not anyone
there was no idiosyncrasy left that colored her light

while the ego was an accident, the self was a substance
the self was more real than a shell that carried a name
she was aware of the fact and thereby received grace

although the self roved between accidents with names
the self was nameless, it was more permanent than a role
it was the source of outpouring love, the spring of courage

the self was not hers to own but was abandoned to God
because *abandonment* was her theme (her *Leitmotiv*)

the self was a drop of being immersed in an ocean of Being
the self was consciousness dissolved in Consciousness
the self was a wave of love traversing a universe of Love
the self moved at the speed of hope with time standing still
the self was a grain of sand, then only a shadow thereof
mostly unrecognized by people but beyond superficiality

in the elated monastery on Mount Carmel she prayed
permit me, o Lord, to console You for ingratitude
and indifference, for the lack of love offered to You
You who are Love cannot be loved enough!
permit me, o Lord, to bring souls to You in perpetuity
to spend my heaven on earth tending your garden

for those who see me i am a teacher or a Queen
ruling their poor lives and explaining their world
for those who see me not i am a humble servant
nudging them along gently on the path to You

for myself i am a grain of sand forever indebted to You
singing your praises, o Lord, until with empty hands
i stand before You for all good things come from You

he was still looking at the spot where the sun had set
behind him the wall of sanctuary radiated the warmth
it had gained from the long hours of afternoon light

she had entered the monastery and asked him to wait
which was easy now because he was void of worries
he had died to the distraction of material confinement
with that realization waves of love overcame him
and he perceived the world in an entirely new order

she made him reconsider all, relive every experience
reevaluate every moment that eternity had on offer
all thoughts became devoted to her, she was the ray
that guided him, she was one with light everlasting

in her he saw God

when she looked at him God was looking at him
it was natural therefore to wish to kneel before her
to disappear before her and to vanish in this love
to merge with this love and become one with her

then there was one soul, one soul for two bodies
then there was one body, one body and one form

he felt insignificant while she was all meaningful
she was representative of the world and its powers
the idea that she noticed him seemed inconceivable
why would a Queen of Heaven, a Bodhisattva saving
worlds be moved by a pair of eyes looking at her?

he knew she responded to the hopes of people
it was her resolve to save each and every soul
to make herself available to sinners and saints
to teach everyone who applied to her in earnest

now in that golden moment after the sunset
he felt deep within that she loved him too
and even that she had always loved him

how can this miracle come to exist? he wondered
how can she love someone who wished to be no one?
her answer was a pointer to the absolute realm

i love you because you wish to be no one, she had said
on a terrace overlooking an emerald southern ocean
in a gentle evening breeze when consorts enrobed her

smiling gently she continued, i love you because
you long to vanish in your—oh so—rational love for me
and for the Eternal Word which springs from heaven

i love you because you hold nothing in reserve
but instead you give all that you have to me
to the Queen of Heaven and therefore to God

then his ego disappeared but his self remained
and renewed the love many times and again
his self was given to her and therefore to God
his self was held by her and therefore by God

the ego strives randomly, the self knows the way
the self becomes one with God, she explained
as a drop of pure water dissolves in the ocean

their embrace was eternal, it was a burning heart
when he held her soul with trembling hands
he touched her self within and thus the world
then they were together in one soul, in one library
discovering unchartered worlds, experiencing uncreated light

does God permit fusion of souls? he had once asked her
while it is the natural aim to strive for oneness with God
what does it mean to fuse with another created substance?
how do we love eternal substances that are less than God?
they have perfection of a kind but not perfection as such

she had replied to his curiosity: two souls fuse in the moment
when they become one with God and thus one with all souls
your desire to be one with me is a symbol for the blessed hope
to become one with God for love is mutual enjoyment in God

7

this had been her answer on the summit of a mountain
they had gained, one that had not been named before
together with her he wanted to learn about all created forms
and see the mesmerizing beauty of the world she ruled

seeing that beauty within her and being aware of it
there was nothing left but to weep with gratitude
to embrace the longing and make it an offer to God

as it grew darker and the evening stars became visible
he prayed by the sanctuary that rested on top of the hill

Lord, forgive me three sins due to my limitation
You are everywhere but i worship You here
You are without form but i worship You in her
You need no praise but i worship You incessantly

5.8

as the evening descended her steps were guided back
to the cathedral of infinity, to the basilica of books
when she entered the church it was a coming home
a step into what was familiar and yet beyond reach

she knew this entry was her last, this time was forever

she advanced between grand columns of eternal books
at half-infinity she found the area delineated by petals
she knelt down and prayed, she removed her shoes
then she prostrated herself before the divine presence

she was alone in the church but one with all souls
the living flame of love forever inextinguishable
within her had given her the confidence to know

if you seek God, God seeks you much more
if you love God, God loves you much more
while no human action can merit His grace
God gives us abundantly without restraint
and His love for us is entirely unconditional

she knew the words written in the books
for the Doctor Mysticus and for Saint Athanasius
as the Father loves the Son, so God loves you
God became man, so we can become God

she contemplated the immensity of these affirmations
which governed the worlds assembled around her

God's unconditional love is poured out for all creatures
however much she loved God His love for her is unmatched
there were those moments when she had not seen Him
there were those heart beats when her soul was distracted

then the prisoner had been waiting unconsoled in the dark
the hungry had been starving deprived of nourishment
the patient had been dying without the light of faith
the despairing had been left without hope of redemption

this is what it means not to love enough
to withhold a fiber of your finite being
the realization of missed opportunities
that existed in the realm made her weep

where were you my Beloved when i failed?
when i could not see you between dark clouds?

i was with you always, came the answer
i was with you from the dawn of time
i will be with you until the end of time

when you did not see me you were not looking
when you did not hear me you were not listening

in trial i was by your side, in moments of joy i held you
in aridity i was making you empty to receive new graces
i was preparing you for new gifts i could bestow on you

know then, my beloved, that i have been with you forever
in the sequence of moments spread out before me as the now

then she was silent in the dome of books

at midnight she prayed

i am infinitely grateful for the works you have done in me
for the graces you have given me absent any merit of mine
you do not give what i deserve, you overlook my iniquity
your justice is mercy and your mercy is love without limit

i am not worthy to raise my voice in your presence
and yet i am speaking to you, o Lord of all worlds

forgive me for asking: where are you, my Lord
when people hurt others, when sin inflicts pain
when ignorance causes harm and suffering?

where are you, my Lord, in moments of malady
of crime and retaliation, of greed and selfishness
that are painfully present in the human trajectory
that i could not prevent despite the light of reason

my beloved soul, the answer is known to you
in those moments i am the perpetual victim
in those moments i am the one who accepts
without complaint the wounds inflicted on me
even in those moments my love is not shaken
and i forgive those who transgress against me

divine love suffers when meeting the temporality of sin
but as human love grows those incidents will be fewer
until they disappear when your love has found me

after those images her prayer became silent
as she had the ability to be silent with God
prayer is something that happened to her
that came from within as the spring of her love

time passed or not in the great dome of books
as she was prostrated motionless or nearly so

her thoughts were fixed on the current of people
moving through time and searching for purpose
here and there a few saints, lovers, or innocents
but most were wanderers in a night of confusion
drifting through the world unguided by love

few knew themselves while many hurt others
they were searching for truth without finding
they were gathering food which did not satisfy

why this confusion, why this lasting torment
if God's love is all present and all embracing?
if the magnificent creation is perfect in conception
why do people commit sin? why is there failure?

freedom, she knew, was not the answer
because true freedom is union with God

freedom is freedom from sin but not possibility to sin
suffering arises when the soul ignores the gifts given

ignorance of God's love and subversion of beauty lead to sin
embracing the virtues as offered by God enables fulfillment
makes this life and the entire creation infinitely beautiful

inflicting suffering is ignorance, committing sin is darkness
choosing distance from God leads to a lack of perspective
where God is, there is no sin! where God is, sin cannot be!

confusion causes worry and fear of temporality
but it is from fragility that we reach for God
that we turn to God that we begin to love God
likewise God reaches for us in the exile of confusion

this mutual desire, this longing, this hope,
this love is the purpose of the whole creation

freedom is freedom to love while sin is failure to love
on this line we can move in two opposite directions
the random walk of love is biased by the grace of God

souls are permitted to love freely else there is no purpose
but if creatures love freely they can also withhold love
or they can turn their love from higher to lower goods

to love a lesser good instead of a higher one is confusion
the highest good is God—our love can be offered to God
but our distraction sometimes prevents us from doing so

before sunrise she thought how can she help people?
what is her mission on earth? in this trajectory?
and not only on this one planet but on all planets
from the beginning of time until the end of time
until the angel sounds the final trumpet...
...or perhaps forever if creation was unlimited

increasingly she was attracted to this idea
it implied that her sacrifice was unending
that the days of her rest would never come

forever she would give herself as a victim of love
as a burning offering over the face of the deep
as a fire ritual that connects her to heaven

if she offered herself a victim, people could see the path
they could turn to her, they could ask her for guidance
they could request a code to find their way toward joy

kneeling before her they would be kneeling before God
who alone can dry their tears and still all their worries
kneeling before God her prayer was silent

they could trust her because she only proclaimed God's love
as she never does her own will she is one with her Beloved
she knew she had to promise herself as a victim of love
and then hold on to that love in every tunnel of darkness

she reached into the pocket that was close to her heart
and took out a letter—offering it with both hands
she placed it on the floor before her and before Him
then she resumed her position in the cathedral of books

i accept your suit, she said, in the dome of infinity
built of the eternal word i promise to be your bride
i will be your Queen and you will be my God
you will be my Lover and i will be your Beloved
i will be your Lover and you will be my Beloved

my commitment to You, o Eternal Word, which is made
here in the cathedral of infinity, in the limitless library
in the garden of philosophy, in the elated monastery
is—by your grace—absolute, unconditional, irresolvable
irreformable and independent of the consent of creatures

make me Yours! remove everything in me that is not You
then she was silent as infinite peace descended

she realized before Him each moment was eternity
before Him even absence of language was language
absence of music was music, absence of time was time

the contents of the letter written by her own hand
written with her own blood spiraled inaudibly upward
through the vast cathedral of books, letters, numbers
merging into a single number, into a single Platonic Form
which was no longer written by her, but was composed
by Him who is author of all books, originator of all Ideas

❀ ❀ ❀

. . .

time is nothing in your eyes, a day is like a thousand years
thus you can in one instant call me to appear before you

in order to live in a single act of perfect love
i offer myself as a victim to your merciful love
consume me incessantly!

let the waves of your tenderness flow into my soul
may i become a martyr of your love, o my God
may this martyrdom after having prepared me
to appear before you finally cause me to die
may my soul take its flight without delay
into the eternal embrace of your merciful love

i want, o my Beloved, at each beat of my heart
renew this offering to you an infinite number of times
until the shadows having disappeared i may be able
to tell you of my Love in an eternal face to face

MOVEMENT
6

6.1

kneeling before the saint she asked for his blessing
passing the door she thought forever and ever

she had no illusion about life in religion
she had no difficulty following the rule
her love was stronger than life or death
love endures all, love achieves all

the desert of the mountain gave her peace
it gave her the ability to find a way within
and a humble teaching which would affirm
the path for others—forever and ever

life is passing before our senses
eternity is advancing in great strides
let us be ready to embrace infinity

after drinking at the fountain of sorrow
we will be refreshed at the spring of joy
then with one look we will understand
what is taking place in our souls

images of this world are fading away
soon we shall see new heavens
more radiant suns will light up
and illuminate ethereal spaces
infinite splendor will arise

immensity will be our domain
with our heavenly Lover we will
sail on unbounded oceans since
infinity has no limit, no ceiling

God's love for us can only
be understood by God alone
God has done foolish things for us
let us do foolish things for God
love is repaid by love alone
only love heals all wounds

i refuse God nothing because
i know that with a single sigh
from my heart i can save souls
oh heaven! when will we be there?

6.3

[Céline writes:]

we were in the august city and i asked
for directions using the foreign language

the man was pleased with my meager attempts
and was forthcoming in answering my questions
meanwhile she looked at me with astonishment
for having endeavored to speak Italian

at the fountain we were told if we threw in a coin
we would be forced to return — we did not throw any

she however would return for her coronation

6.4

scholars of the order found
the letter she carried on her heart
at the ceremony in the cathedral of infinity

My Lord and my Beloved, prevent me
from committing the slightest fault
may i never seek anything other than you
may i never find anything other than you

may creatures be nothing to me
may i be nothing to them
may you be everything to me!
may things of the earth never trouble my soul
never disturb my peace!

Light of my life, i ask for peace, i ask for love
love that is not me but you, infinite love without limits
may i die for you because love is stronger than death

give me grace to fulfill the vows to perfection
make me understand always how your beloved
should behave before you and the world

never let me be a burden to people
let nobody be distracted by me
let no one be occupied with me
let them see me as your servant
let them treat me as a grain of sand

may your will be done in me perfectly
may i reach the place you have prepared for me

allow me to save souls and bring them to you
pardon me if i ever say or think anything
i should not—my only aim is to love you!

6.5

since souls rarely allow God to rest peacefully in them
i wish to imagine He delights over the repose i offer Him
when He sleeps within me i do not disturb Him
when He leaves me alone to navigate the waves of life
without His consolation i do not awake Him

i am far from being a saint, if i was i should not rejoice
at my aridity but attribute it to my lack of fervor

i should be desolate over falling asleep during prayer but i am not
children sleep in their parents' arms, so do i in my Father's embrace
God is always present in my heart, He acts within me as He wills
He makes me think of all that He desires me to accomplish

in the morning of my eternal vows i was flooded
with a river of peace which surpassed all understanding
my union with Jesus was effected without mighty signs
now i was a Queen who could obtain favors for souls

i had offered myself to God entirely, so He could do
His will in me perfectly without selfishness distracting me

yet this beautiful day passed just as the saddest one
because each day has a tomorrow
i removed my crown and placed it at Her feet

in the evening i gazed at the stars in the firmament
i was thinking one day this beautiful heaven will open
to my ravished eyes and i will be able to embrace
my Beloved in the light of an eternal bliss

fear makes me recoil while love gives me wings
i realized that without love all works are for nothing

God showered gifts upon me without me asking for them
but they did not make me vain, they drew me closer to Him
He alone is unchangeable, He alone fulfills my desires
He gives hundredfold in this life to souls who love Him

i have no desire except to love God until folly
love alone attracts me, abandonment guides me
i have no other compass in the world
i cannot ask for anything with fervor
except that God's will is done in my soul

committing infidelities grieves me but love erases them
love establishes profound peace in the depths of my heart

how much light have i drawn from the works
of John of the Cross who is my spiritual nourishment
now i know that the kingdom of God is within us

God teaches me without the sound of His gentle voice
i have never heard Him speak, yet He is within me always
guiding me and inspiring me what to do and where to go

if all creatures had received the wonderful graces
God lavished on me He would be loved universally
then through love not fear no one would cause Him pain

but not all souls proceed along the same path
differences are necessary to honor God in distinct ways
i was granted the favor of contemplating His infinite mercy
and through it adore the other divine properties

but all divine perfections are resplendent with love
therefore we know that His justice is clothed in love
what a joy that God is just, that He considers our fragility!

what should i fear then? will the infinitely just God
who pardons the prodigal son with so much kindness
not also be just toward me who am with Him always?

on the feast of the Holy Trinity i received the grace
to understand how much God desires to be loved by us

thinking of a soul who offered herself as victim of God's justice
to alleviate punishment of sinners by drawing it upon herself
i realized this offering was generous but i was not attracted to it

from the depth of my heart i cried: my God, will your justice
alone find souls willing to immolate themselves as victims?
does not your love which is rejected long for them too?
many hearts who could receive your love turn to creatures
seeking happiness from them with their miserable affection
they do this rather than throwing themselves into your arms

will your disdained love remain closed up in your heart?
if you were to find souls offering themselves to your love
you would consume them rapidly without holding back

your love fills the heavens and desires to set souls on fire
therefore let me be a victim of your love, o Lord!
consume my offering with the fire of your divine love

when making this offer rivers of grace flooded my soul
since that day love surrounds me wherever i am

each moment your merciful love renews me, purifies my soul,
leaves no trace of sin in me—love sanctifies more than fear!
how sweet is the way of love! how i want to apply myself
to following the will of God with greatest self-surrender

you wonder how the story of the little flower will end?
will she be plucked soon and transplanted to other shores?
i do not know but i am sure God's mercy will accompany her

she will never cease blessing her mother who offered her to Jesus
she will rejoice eternally at being one of the flowers in her crown
with this mother she will sing forever the canticle of Love

6.6

o God, blessed Trinity, i desire to love you and make you loved
i desire to work for you and for your Holy Church
by saving souls on earth, by liberating all who are suffering

i desire to accomplish your will perfectly and reach
the place you have prepared for me in your kingdom
i desire to be a saint, but i am aware of my helplessness
thus i implore you, o my God, to be my sanctity

since you loved me so much as to give me your only son
as my savior and my spouse his infinite merits are mine
i offer them to you with gladness begging you to look at me
only through the face of Jesus and his loving heart

i offer you too the merits of the saints, their acts of love
and those of the holy angels, i offer you, o Holy Trinity,
the love and merits of the Blessed Virgin, my Mother
to her i abandon my offering begging her to present it to you

her divine son, my beloved spouse, told us in his mortal life:
whatever you ask the father in my name he will give to you
thus i am certain that you will grant my wishes since i know
the more you want to give me the more you make me desire

in my heart are immense desires and it is with confidence
that i ask you to come and take possession of my soul

i cannot receive communion as often as i wish but i ask you
to remain in me as in a tabernacle without ever leaving me

i want to console you for the ingratitude of the world
i beg of you to take away my freedom to displease you

if through weakness i fall, may your divine glance
purify my soul at once and consume my imperfections
like the fire that transforms everything into itself

i thank you, beloved Savior, for the gifts you have granted me
for the grace of making me carry the crucible of suffering
with joy i shall contemplate you on the last day of my life

since you deigned to give me a share in your precious cross
i hope in heaven to resemble you and see in my glorified body
the stigmata of your passion

after earth's exile i hope to go and enjoy you in the fatherland
but i do not want to lay up any treasures for heaven
i want to work for love alone with the purpose of pleasing you,
of consoling your heart and saving souls who love you eternally

in the evening of this life i shall appear before you
with empty hands because i do not ask you to count my works
since our justice is stained in your eyes i wish to be clothed
in your Justice and receive from your Love eternal possession
of Yourself—i want no other crown but You, my Beloved

time is nothing in your eyes, a day is like a thousand years
thus you can in one instant call me to appear before you

in order to live in a single act of perfect love
i offer myself as a victim to your merciful love
consume me incessantly!

let the waves of your tenderness flow into my soul
may i become a martyr of your love, o my God
may this martyrdom after having prepared me
to appear before you finally cause me to die
may my soul take its flight without delay
into the eternal embrace of your merciful love

i want, o my Beloved, at each beat of my heart
renew this offering to you an infinite number of times
until the shadows having disappeared i may be able
to tell you of my Love in an eternal face to face

6.7

sitting on a stool in her cell she wrote in the book of life
a single lamp illuminated her pen gliding over the paper

you have asked for a souvenir of my retreat which is probably my last
it is a joy for me to come and speak to you who are doubly my sister
you lent me your voice promising that i wished to serve Jesus alone

this child whom you offered to God who speaks to you this evening
is the one who loves you as a child loves its mother

dear sister, you wish to hear the secrets Jesus confides to me
however i realize that He reveals those secrets to you too
for you have taught me how to gather divine instructions

nevertheless i will stammer words though i know it is impossible
for the human tongue to express what the heart can barely grasp

i am not rich in consolations for i have none on earth
God teaches me in silence without making His voice heard

only rarely words come to me which console me such as this one:
"here is a teacher i give you, he will teach you all you must do!
i want you to read the book of life which contains the science of love"

the science of love!—the term resounds sweetly in my soul
i desire to study this science! having given all my riches for it
i esteem having given nothing as the bride in the sacred canticles
love is the only good i desire, love makes us acceptable to God

Jesus showed me the road leading to the divine furnace:
it is the surrender of a child sleeping in its parents' arms
whoever is little let him come to me, speaks the Holy Spirit
the same Spirit says: to her who is little mercy will be shown

the prophet Isaiah proclaims: "on the last day God will feed
his flock like a shepherd, he shall gather together the lambs
with his arm taking them up in his bosom"

the same prophet whose gaze was plunged into eternal depths
cried out in the Lord's name: "as one whom a mother caresses
so i will comfort you, then you will be carried at the breasts
and upon knees they will caress you"—after listening to those
words there is nothing left but to weep with gratitude and love

if all weak souls felt what the least of souls (my own) then feels
no one would despair of reaching the summit of the mount of love
God does not demand greatness but surrender and gratitude

the Almighty has said: "i do not take the goats from your flocks
for all beasts of the forest are mine, the cattle on the hills and
the oxen, i know all the fowls of the air—if i was hungry
i would not tell you for the world is mine in its fullness"

therefore offer to God sacrifices of love and of thanksgiving

the same God who declares He has no need to tell us
when He is hungry asked the Samaritan woman for water
when He said, give me to drink, it was the love of the creature
the Lord of the universe was seeking—He is thirsty for love!

Jesus is parched when meeting ingratitude and indifference
few hearts surrender to him and accept His Love

how fortunate are you, dear sister, to understand these secrets!
if you wrote down all you knew of those revelations we would
have beautiful pages to read but i know that you prefer
to keep the King's secrets in the bottom of your heart

yet to me you say: it is honorable to publish the works of the Most High
you are right to maintain silence and in obedience to you i write

how powerless i am to express in language the treasures of heaven
there are so many horizons and nuances of infinite variety that only
the palette of the celestial painter will be able to furnish me—after
the night of this life—with colors capable of depicting the marvels

you have asked me dear sister to write about my dream
and my little doctrine as you have chosen to call it

pardon me if you will find my expressions exaggerated
this is due to my poor style because i assure you there is
no exaggeration in my soul—within all is calm and peace

when writing these words i shall address them to Jesus
which makes it easier for me to express my simple thoughts
but it does not prevent them from being poorly composed

Jesus, who can describe the love with which you guide souls?
a storm was raging in me since the radiant feast of Easter
thinking of mysterious dreams which are granted to others
i told myself they must be sweet consolations

in the evening seeing the clouds which covered heaven
my soul thought that blessed dreams were not for her
then she fell gently asleep in the midst of the storm

at the glimmer of dawn i was in a gallery in a dream
there were several persons present at a distance

when i saw three Carmelites in their long veils i realized
that they had come from heaven—in my heart i cried
how happy i would be if i could see the face of one of them!

as though my prayer was heard the tallest came toward me
i fell to my knees, she raised her veil and covered me with it

i recognized Anne of Jesus, foundress of Carmel in France,
friend of Saint Teresa: her face was of immaterial beauty
suffused with a gentle light that shone right from within
i cannot express the joy that overcame me at this moment

seeing myself so gently loved i pronounced those words:
"Mother i beg you, tell me whether God will leave me
on earth for a long time or will He get me soon?"

smiling tenderly she whispered, "soon, soon, i promise"

i added, "Mother please tell me if God is asking more of me
than my little actions and desires? or is He content with me?"

the saint's face took on an expression more tender than before
her look and caresses were the sweetest of answers, she said
"God asks nothing else of you! He is content, very content"

after embracing me with the love of the kindest of mothers
i saw her leave—then suddenly i remembered my sisters
and i wanted to ask favors for them—but alas i awoke

the storm no longer raged, heaven was calm and serene
i believed there was a heaven and this heaven was peopled
with souls who loved me who considered me their child

the impression remains in my heart and all the more
because until then i was indifferent to Anne of Jesus
i had never invoked her in prayer, the thought of her
never came to my mind except when others spoke of her

when i understood how much she loved me although i had
been indifferent toward her, my heart was filled with love
not only for her but for all inhabitants of heaven

o my Beloved! this grace was the prelude to other graces
you wished to bestow upon me! allow me then, my only Love,
to recall them to you today on the anniversary of our union!

pardon me, if i am unreasonable in expressing my desires
to be a Carmelite, to be your spouse, to be a mother of souls
by union with you—should this not suffice?

although these privileges sum up my vocation i find further calls
i feel the vocation of a warrior, priest, apostle, doctor, martyr
i feel the desire of carrying out the most heroic deeds for you
within my soul is the courage to die in defense of the Church

i feel the vocation of a priest: with what pious love, o Jesus
would i hold you in my hands when at my voice you descend
from heaven, with what outpouring love would i give you to souls

i wish to enlighten souls as did prophets and doctors
as an apostle of your love i wish to travel the earth
to plant your glorious cross on all continents and islands

i long to be a missionary: from beginning of time until
the end i want to shed my blood for you to the last drop!
martyrdom was the dream of my youth and this dream
has grown with me over the years in Carmel's cloisters

what do you reply to my follies? is any soul smaller than mine?

to find some kind of answer i opened the epistles of Paul
i read that not all can be apostles, prophets, or doctors
that instead the church is composed of different parts
the eye cannot be the hand at one and the same time

the answer was clear but did not grant me peace
yet as Mary Magdalene found what she was seeking
by stooping down and looking into the tomb
so i abasing myself to the depths of my nothingness
raised myself so high that i was able to find

without being discouraged i read on until this sentence
consoled me: strive after the better gifts! i will now
point out to you a more excellent way . . . then the apostle
explains how the perfect gifts are nothing without love
love is the way that leads to God! and finally i had rest!

considering the mystical body of the church i had not found
myself in any of the members described by the great apostle
although i had strongly desired to see myself in all of them

love was the key to my vocation: if the church had a body
composed of parts then the most noble could not be lacking

so i understood that the church had a heart and this heart
was forever burning with love; it was love alone that made
the church act, if love ever became extinct apostles would not
preach the gospel, martyrs would not shed their blood

in delirious joy i cried out: o Jesus, my vocation is love!
i have found my place in the church and You have given
this place to me: in the heart of the church, i am love!
thus i shall be everything and my dream will be realized

why speak of delirious joy? this expression is not exact
for it was the calm peace of the navigator seeing the port

o luminous beacon of love, i know how to reach you
i have found the secret of possessing your flame
i am only a powerless child, yet my weakness gives me
the boldness of offering myself as a victim of love

in the past only spotless victims were acceptable to God
to satisfy divine justice perfect victims were needed
but the law of love has succeeded the law of fear

love has chosen me as victim, an imperfect creature
this choice is worthy of love: for love lowers itself
to nothingness, it transforms nothingness into fire

6.8

for me too will come the last night when i sing
your mercies in this exile, then i want to say to You:

"my God, i have glorified you on earth
i have finished the work you have asked me to do
now glorify me with yourself with the glory
i had with you before the world existed

i have manifested your name to those you have given me
i have passed on your word and they have received it
they have learned that all i have is from you
they know the truth: that i have come from you

i pray for those you have given me because they are yours
all things that are mine are yours and yours are mine
i am no longer in the world for i am coming to you
Father, keep in your name those you have given me

these words i speak in the world that they may have joy
i have given them your word and the world has hated them
they are not of the world even as i am not of the world

i do not pray that you take them out of the world
but keep them from evil; not for them alone i pray
but for all those who believe through their word

Father, i will that where i am they will be with me
that they may see the glory which you have given me
because you have loved me from the beginning of time

i have made your name known and will make it known
your love for me may be in them and i in them"

is it too bold to repeat your words?
you have always permitted me to be bold before you!

you have said what is yours is mine—your words are mine
i use them to draw upon souls the favors of our Father

i have never desired anything else but to love you
i seek no other glory for Love alone attracts me!
your Love has grown with me over time in this exile
now it is a wide ocean whose depths i cannot fathom

my love leaps toward Yours, it would like to fill its depth
but it is only a drop of dew which is lost in the open sea
to love You as You love me i have to borrow Your Love
and only then i would be at rest in Your arms

hand me lever and fulcrum so i lift the world for You
what Archimedes did not obtain the saints have received
the Lord has given them a fulcrum: Himself alone
and a lever: prayer which burns with the fire of love

thus the saints can lift the world toward You
and they continue to do so until the end of time

6.9

You have smiled at me in the morning of my life and now it is evening
choose me for Yourself remove everything in me that is not You

she brought light to light everlasting
she was a beacon of light showing the way

her life was not easy because it saw torment and pain
she was joined to all people who roamed in the dark
she made herself available to liberate all suffering souls
she knew physical malady, darkness, and humiliation

God's beloved was not spared the afflictions of temporality
as she wanted to be one with all souls she refused privilege

to help those who are in pain you must know pain
to feed those who are hungry you must know hunger
to console those who despair you must know despair
to bring to God those who are far you must feel distance

thus her choice was made at the beginning of time
she did not exempt herself from pain, hunger, despair
instead she embraced them and she carried her cross

she was very deep now in that valley of pain
she was present to every suffering soul and body
she consoled those who were in confusion and despair
on her glorified body began to shine the stigmata of passion

and yet the closer she came to the last moment
the more she recognized that any distance from Him
was not only entirely unbearable but also unbridgeable

the last divide you cannot close, the last step you cannot make
then she saw that no single step of her life she had done alone
when she had missed consolation God had been fully present
then there was only one set of footprints in the sands of time
in the spiritual night of the soul she had removed her shoes
since she was carried along in the arms of her Beloved

in the sacred afternoon hour when the air of this earth
eluded her for a long agony she extended her beautiful arms
supported by her sisters—but her calvary continued

in the evening of her life in that last moment
when she was tormented by temptations against hope
confronted by nothingness but still holding on to love
God lifted her weakness and carried her over the last divide

oh my God, i love you! she cried out

open the doors! a voice exclaimed
but she heard those words no more
there was commotion in the room
the sister of the eucharist rushed forward
and lifted a candle before her eyes
to see what they were seeing

but they were just wide open and ravishingly beautiful

MOVEMENT
7

7.1

of whom are we reading? she asked the librarian
he looked up but he did not answer her question

he said, do not seek suffering for its own sake
but if you embrace suffering that cannot be avoided
then it will transform your life and that of others

do you understand me?

i am not sure, she replied

looking at the world we find suffering even without sin
God could have written any book but he wrote this one

tragedy can be a theme even in a world that is beautiful
tragedy does not negate sanctity nor exclude goodness
it rather brings them about and makes them the essence

if we are in a world where the good acts as a servant
tragedy remains a possibility which we have to accept
yet the minion's role is crucial: in fragility and darkness
she shines most splendidly toward the light everlasting

the crucible of suffering which arises in partial light
becomes a preparation for the day of eternity

sanctity is goodness given in the absence of certitude
sanctity is reason to hope even if we encounter despair

comedy is not absent here but is not the dominant theme
in recreation she was joyful as she can be in acts of heaven

are you referring to her of whom we have read? she asked

she could make her sisters laugh, the librarian answered

comedy and tragedy are mingled but they do not recombine
their colors remain separate creating ever moving patterns
tragedy prevails in temporality as its effects are in time

perhaps they are on different stages, she offered

how often were you moments too late? he suddenly asked
how many cities have burned? how many heroes succumbed?

what are you talking about? she wondered

you want to save all souls but have you?

only God saves souls, she replied, i am a mere grain of sand
but the mercies of the Lord i sing, the glory of God i praise!

stars in heaven outnumber grains of sand on earth, he said

but what about books? she asked
are there more books in this library than stars in heaven?

let us continue, he suggested, for it is evening

7.2

love your enemies! the librarian said
good father, i have no enemies, she replied

if there are people, who harm me, who destroy
what i have gathered i do not see them as enemies
they act under confusion, they are not filled by love
evidently they do not know what they are doing

if they were aware of light they would not hurt me
since they walk in darkness i want to help them
i pray that God may restore them to their love
i show them my love so they can be healed

as we have read, where there is no love
you must give love and you will draw love

❁ ❁ ❁

love your enemies! the librarian said
good father, i have no enemies, she replied

those that hurt my body do not reach my inner self
because i alone am the guardian of my soul

they break a shell, burn a house, destroy my work
but i am only my soul which they cannot touch
hurting me they harm their own soul—i pray for them
nothing evil can happen to a good person

❁ ❁ ❁

love your enemies, the librarian said
good father, i have no enemies, she replied

everything that confronts me is willed by God
on my knees i thank the Lord for His graces each day
if people trespass against my material instantiation
they are permitted by God to bring food for my soul

if God deigns that i receive injustice before the world
my heart rejoices because the Lord permits me to grow
in those instances i am especially blessed before people
and the love for the Lord consumes me fervently

praise and glory belong to God alone
the soul cannot grow on those foods
but humiliation makes the soul rejoice
and rise toward the door of heaven

all i have is from God and goes back to God
my only desire is to make God loved on earth

my desire is to kindle love in the hearts of all people
help those who are in pain, feed those who are hungry
my food is love, i am love, it is love that moves me
in the edifice of the church, my mother, i am love

God does not need me: while i devote my life to Him
many others can take my role and be better servants
i am a grain of sand but i do know that He loves me
i give myself to His love and in Him alone i trust

He allows me to console Him
He permits me to bring souls to Him
He asks me to be bold before Him

He has loved me from the beginning of time
and i have promised to be His bride

He grants that my will be done in heaven
as i have never done my will on earth

7·3

good father, how many books are in this library? she asked

my light, he replied, there are infinitely many books

does it contain all books that are combinatorically possible?

oh no, he laughed, our library is not one of those

there are other libraries? she asked

of course, he answered, there are many libraries

please enlighten me about libraries and books

certainly, my Lady, he leaned back in his chair

first let us ask: what is a library? what a book?
these questions seem innocent but they are not
permit me to propose: a library is a set of books
thus a library applies the concept of set to books

we can say that a set is a collection of objects
some objects are in the set while others are not
some books are in the library while others are not

we know that a set is a mathematical object
since mathematical objects are real and abstract
we conclude that libraries are real and abstract

some libraries are instantiated in the material realm
but this minor footnote need not concern us now
those material libraries are fragile, they have a habit
of burning down or being destroyed and abandoned
they rarely survive for more than . . . a thousand years

real libraries are forever! do you see where i am going?

probably, she replied

next let us ask: what is a book? he continued

a book is a mathematical object, a longish number
but not too long if someone is supposed to read it

we can use any set of symbols to present that number
we can use the organic alphabet of a human language
or transform letters into binary code or anything else
as long as it conforms to good taste and simplicity

simplicity is the mother of good taste, she inserted

an integer remains an integer, a book remains a book
a book remains an integer, an integer remains a book
integers are forever, books are forever, he continued

the librarian derived great pleasure from pronouncing
those profundities which reaffirmed simple truth

are the sets of books and integers equivalent? she asked

probably, my Lady, he said nodding in affirmation
unless you seek to constrain the notion of book
because some wish to argue a book must make sense

pedantic scholars define the concept of book that way
more open-minded ones equate books and integers

the latter hold "making sense" is an ill-defined notion
since many well intended books make not much sense

i do not blame them, he added with a mischievous smile

the scholars or the books? she wondered

you can choose either side, it makes no difference
the number of books is the same: countably infinite

we are in the wonderful world of discrete infinity!
he exclaimed a dream-like expression on his face

the unfathomable richness of discrete infinity
gives us this unbearable lightness of being
that shines forth here in our beautiful library

my Lady, at this moment pause to consider
that binary expressions can be enumerated
that formulations in the reals can be solved
but equations with those sacred integers...
this is where the human touches the divine

and we are blessed with languages
that generate for us discrete infinity

in competence to be sure, he added
in competence not in performance!
i am never talking of performance
why should anyone care about that?

humans have combinatorial tools for
generating infinitely many sentences
—in competence, he re-emphasized

competence is a mathematical object
he said meandering in his daydream
we conclude that our competence is real
while all our performance is accidental

performance is electrochemical noise of neurons
a meddling of billiard balls in a confined skull...

the line of the narrative seemed to have slipped
from his cards which he still held close to his chest

where are we? he suddenly asked

books and integers, she reminded him

oh yes! my Lady, forgive me, i got distracted
it is similar to sieving integers for prime numbers
there are many integers which are not prime
and yet the two sets have the same cardinality

there are as many integers as there are primes
we have countably infinitely many of both

i understand that by now, she answered

as numbers subsist in our beloved Platonic heaven
he continued, so we find sets of numbers there
books exist in this reality and thus sets of books
therefore also libraries, not just one but many

there are many more libraries than books
many more libraries than we can count

uncountably infinitely many libraries, she said

yes! there are as many libraries as real numbers
a library is a language, here we are in one library
in a particular one, in one of many, he replied

i am the librarian here, he said pondering his fate
which suddenly seemed extraordinary to him!
a librarian is a friend, a linguist, a philosopher,
a mathematician! it all comes back to mathematics

good father, this idea brings me to my next question:
which books are in this library? what does it represent?

he was quiet for a moment, his face became focused
it seemed that he managed to collect his thoughts

my Lady, not every library can be explained, he said
we have established there are as many books as integers
and that there are as many libraries as real numbers

asking what a specific library represents is equivalent
to computing the real number that indicates this library

a real number is computable if there exists an algorithm
that can provide its digits—since algorithms are countable
few reals can be computed, few libraries can be explained
for most libraries we are at a loss when someone asks:
what do they represent? he suddenly seemed tired

but for this one here? are we at a loss for this library?
she asked pressing the point which was important to her
we cannot be at a loss, right? else why would i be here?

cogito ergo sum, he answered

my Lady, we are not out of resource, he affirmed
when trying to engage that particular question

you can think of a librarian as representing an answer
the presence of a librarian indicates there is an answer
if there was no answer you would not have found me

for this our beloved library three answers are available
and i am pleased to give them to you one after the other

i have strained your patience for too long already
though you might agree we are not pressed for time
as time indicates change and moves events in space
books do not change but remain still as time passes

do you feel this, my Lady? he asked

i can feel it in some moments, she said

for the first answer permit me to commence thus:
long ago a rumor circulated in Athens that Plato
had written a book about the Form of the Good
according to that legend Plato had responded
that such a book could never have been written

that story always amused me!

why is this, good father?

because the first answer i can provide is as follows:
all books in this library are about the Form of the Good

the books in these hallowed halls reveal how the Form
acts within people, and how she propels time in her wake
how she governs the will, how she illuminates other forms
how she infuses material realms, how she brings us to God

all books in this library are about the Form of the Good
yet no single book reaches full explanatory adequacy
there is not one book that entirely reveals her essence
i guess the impossibility of such was pointed out by Plato

coming closer to understanding the Form of the Good
requires the experience of a life in the material realm
with its highs and lows, with temptations against hope
but the library is the tool that permits this approach

all books in this library are about the Form of the Good
this assertion represents the first answer for you

then our library is a precious resource, she remarked
the world would derive benefit from gaining access
what can we do to make the library widely known?

be patient, my Lady, you have received one answer
but two more are still waiting to be exposed

she arose and walked slowly through the librarian's room
she screened the tall shelves, the tidy alignment of books
while the library had endless corridors and grand rooms
it had always seemed to her that all books could directly
be accessed from this one abode resting in its very center

for the second answer let me ask you a question, he said
what is it that brings people to the Form of the Good?
which force leads us to her? which principle guides us?

in one place on a shelf she saw the image of a woman
she had noticed it before but now it seemed to her
the picture could move between places in the room
it was sometimes in one location and then in another
the image was a photograph from early days of the art

the depicted woman was a religious of a holy order
she held a rosary with a crucifix dangling from it
over a brown homespun she wore a white cloak
which touched the ground because she was kneeling
a cross behind her leaned against an overgrown wall
flowers provided accents, the nun was looking at her

she turned to face the librarian and said, it is love!

you are correct, my Lady, love is the attracting force
love emanating from the Form draws us to her forever

how do you define love for those eager to learn?

in my own poor words? she wondered

that would be entirely appropriate, he replied

love is the desire to be devoted to everlasting beauty
to everlasting goodness, to the source of all perfection
love is the ability to keep the rule, the wish to remove
all selfishness, the willingness to accept all sacrifice
love brings us to the highest Form, all love is for God

well said, he commended her, the second answer is:
all books in our esteemed library are about Love

i see why the two answers are compatible, she replied
without love you cannot see or know what is good
if you are not guided by the Form you cannot love
therefore the one is never found without the other

very good, my Lady, the librarian congratulated her
what if we put it thus: Love is the subject of the library
the Form of the Good is the principle behind the subject

this is too scholastic for me, she answered with a laugh
but nevertheless acceptable once i get accustomed to it

and what is your third answer? she asked expectantly

she was descending stairs leading away from him
her heart was beating violently, she was in turmoil
she did not want to leave! she preferred to stay!

because who would read to him from now on?
which human voice was to illuminate his cell?
she wanted to return! yet his advice was clear
his arguments were reasonable and compelling

the librarian had told her it was her responsibility
to act in the world, to participate in the creation
while it was not in her power to finish the work
she was not free to abstain from it either

he emphasized, while it seemed a farewell to her
it was not one for him, he would remain near her
because of the books she was present to him
he could delight in her works in perpetuity

since her path was reflected in the written word
the library revealed to him wherever she strove
her fate was to serve a line that was never to break
and his to be a librarian of a fine collection of books

before leaving him whom she considered to be a saint
an elect of God, she knelt and asked for his blessing
only then she got up and walked away from him

after descending more stairs she reached a door
in secret she hoped it might be locked but it was not
the door was open and it was a one-way passage

since the decision was hers in appearance
she paused and prayed—for how long?
we do not know since time diffuses slowly
time waited on the other side of the door

finally she got up and took a deep breath
voluntarily she stepped over the threshold
some of her memories fainted in this farewell
while others renewed in the cycle of samsara

❀ ❀ ❀

it was an early morning before the song of birds
vague colors began to separate from the shadows

thou art in my eyes, thou art in my mind
thou art in my thoughts — then where am i not?

where am i? she wondered

she was in a tall forest, mist hung in treetops
her feet were cold and her clothes were damp
her hair was glittering with faint morning dew

she held a tall wooden staff in her hand
a small bag was wrapped around her shoulder
its sparse contents were known to her:
a timeworn crucifix, a clay bowl, a japa mala
dried rose petals and the hidden face of God

there was a single path between towering trees
she followed her destiny and walked steadily
her own body — though young — was exhausted

for how long had she been traversing this world?
her hope was to find people whom she could serve

the path crossed a stream cascading from mountains
she knelt down and drank the life-giving icy water
lifting it with both hands she poured it over her head
she washed her face in its purity — it was a baptism

a missionary of love in a foreign land? she wondered
even if this was the case all dominions belong to God
and my mission is to make God loved in this world
however He deigns to use me i want to be ready to act

she resolved to withhold no sacrifice from God
to give Him everything without any hesitation
to abandon herself entirely to His Love and Mercy
to move her soul beyond all confines of selfishness

she looked at her staff which made her smile
was it a shepherd's tool to fight off wild animals?
or a bishop's crosier to keep her flock together?
would she appear before God holding this staff
or carrying a foot warmer as on winter days?

she was a missionary now as she had hoped to be
a missionary of Love spreading the good news
she continued on the path feeling meek in the world
even the nearly empty bag seemed heavy to her

in the evening twilight she found a shepherd's hut
which stood alone under trees and appeared deserted
she observed it from afar then walked around it twice
she wondered if it would do as a shelter for the night

the door creaked as she slowly opened it
inside the hut she found no furniture
she saw worn tools and stacks of dry grass
she noted two separate compartments
she resolved to sleep in one of them
wrapped in her coat huddled in the hay

she took great care to cause no disturbance
her aim was to leave the hut in the morning
exactly as she had found it in the evening
she hoped the owners—whoever they were—
would not mind her using it for one night

before she fell asleep she prayed for them
and then for all people that they would find
calm peace and lasting happiness in their lives
that they would use their earthly existence
to practice true virtue and to bring forth love

she pleaded for the souls of all departed beings
that they were blessed with the beatific vision
and everlasting union with the source of all joy

she prayed for souls roaming other worlds
which she imagined orbiting distant suns
that were loved and upheld by the same God

her prayers became slow and then void of words
until sleep embraced her as the arms of a beloved

love everlasting granted that she was never alone
in that night as in others she knelt in utter devotion
before the absolute light that illuminates all souls

✸ ✸ ✸

she had slept for a few hours when suddenly
she was torn from the realm of silent adoration
there were steps! at once she was fully awake!
her eyes stared into the darkness as she listened

these were no animal steps, no searching wolf
no hungry bear, no grazing deer, but human steps!
human steps were advancing toward the hut

she waited—then there was nothing—no sound
she was holding her breath as silence descended
had the imagined steps been the echo of a dream?
her heart raced as some long moments passed

when she finally concluded that she had only dreamt
hinges squeaked, the door opened, someone entered
then the door closed again, someone was in the room

who has entered? who is here? she wondered
what a dark night of the senses . . . or of the soul

what should she do now? wait or reveal her presence?
speak or be silent? neither choice seemed promising
the hut was small, she was trapped within

after some hesitation she elected to speak
aiming for a calm voice she uttered those words:

whoever you are, wanderer of the night
may God bless you and protect your journey!
you are finding a house at peace but not empty

a quick turn was indicative of astonishment
but afterwards the room fell into silence again
she held her breath listening for the other

who was her visitor concealed by darkness?
a thief in the night? a ranger found off guard?
a shadow from the past? or a poet of no words?

after some silence she decided to speak again
once more she was hoping to sound courageous

do not worry, my friend, do not be distraught
i have come into this world to bring peace
i am not here to judge but i am here to serve
may the peace of the Lord be with you!

and with your spirit! came a meek reply

she recognized a male voice youthful by sound
but subject to tremor which revealed agitation

then the intruder resumed, forgive me, my lady
i did not expect anyone to be present in this hut
please accept my apology for this uncivil entry
i am intending no harm, i will leave you at once

the voice was refined, the words were learned
the visitor opened the door resolved to withdraw

hold on, good sir, she said, i am not in my own place
while foxes have holes i have nowhere to lay my head
it is i who must apologize for causing an imposition
if this hut belongs to you i will leave it immediately

be assured, my Lady, this barn is not owned by me
i have come here before and always found it empty
even if it was my place i would gladly leave it to you
as shelter for the night or for any duration you need

may i propose to remain outside in some proximity
and be a faithful guard who watches over your sleep?

good sir, i am grateful, for your chivalrous offer
but i am hesitating to accept it for this night is cold

suddenly a ray of moonlight fell through a crack
of the withered roof into the interior of the hut
she decided to employ this fleeting opportunity

could you do me the favor of moving slightly
into that beam of light yonder, she proposed

he understood her request and obeyed at once
then standing in the faint light he removed
his woven cap and held it in his hands

he lowered his eyes refraining from gazing
into the dark where he supposed her to be

she saw his face while he could not see hers
the darkness of the room enveloped her features
while the ivory moonlight illuminated his

what is your station in life, sir? she asked him

i am a weaver's son, he replied

your father is a weaver?

my beloved mother is a weaver
my father has left this earthly exile long ago

i am very sorry to hear this, she said

i was three years old when it happened
i have lost a brother too—life has not been easy
i have a surviving brother whom i treasure on earth
i am trying to be of use to him and to my mother
they are the greatest gifts God has given me

she was silent pondering the fate of the young man
who stood before her in the ray of moonlight

i feel a strong vocation, he continued, and i wish
to devote my life to God to make Him loved on earth
i am eager to study and to join a religious order

good sir, she said warmly, your intentions are noble
i sincerely hope that God will grant your wishes
if you seek God, God seeks you much more

i will treasure those beautiful words, he replied

now i beg you to make your bed for the night
in the opposite corner—though this hut is small
it can easily accommodate both of us, she offered

my Lady, please forgive me but i may serve you better
and cause less inconvenience if i rested outside nearby
then i can watch the door lest another visitor comes
and ventures to disturb your sleep which is precious

sir, the night is chilly and i worry for your health
for myself i have decided to shelter within this hut
how could i then ask of you to remain in the cold?
it would be hypocrisy to impose on others
those burdens we do not choose for ourselves

i give you my consent to rest inside, she said
it causes me no impudence and no worry
if you look closely, she continued, the hut has
two compartments that are quite separate

in my Father's house are many rooms, she added

he was silent, after some consideration he said
your consent once given is your command
i oblige with gratitude, i endeavor to be quiet

clouds covered the moon, the ray of light vanished
it was a dark night again within the hut and beyond
but for flames of love that had been kindled in hearts

he settled in the corner she had assigned to him
then he was inaudible and motionless in an instant
but into the silence of darkness his prayer was:
continue to speak to me you powers of heaven!

a moment later he heard her say, if you wish
you may tell me more about your vocation

my resolution is not fully formed, he answered
but it is love that draws me, my vocation is love

your vocation is love! she repeated
her eyes were wide open in the dark

yes, madam, it is love—with all humility

this is an excellent vocation, she replied
it is impossible to fathom a better one

suddenly she smiled, a weaver's son! of course!
how slow i am tonight! the walk has exhausted me

collecting memories of heaven, she said
love is repaid by love alone
wounds of love are healed by love
when evening comes we will be examined on love

who gifts me those words? he asked

a grain of sand, she replied

he realized he was beginning to tremble within
what an intensity of life! what a fire of devotion!
what is your name in the world? he asked

not Genevieve, she thought but remained silent

her heart reached out to that nightly visitor
deep within the library she searched for words
that would guide him on his journey to God

she knew his path was not an easy one
but he would draw many souls in his wake
he would be declared great among people

in the library, in her memory, in her soul
she found books she had been looking for
she turned pages with quivering hands
her fingers touched the smooth surface

o living flame of love, she read
o living flame of love, she spoke
o living flame of love, she sang

o living flame of love
which woundest my soul in its deepest center
if it be your will tear the veil of this encounter

o delightful wound, o delicate touch
o gentle hand that tastes of eternal life

o lamp of fire in whose splendor caverns of feeling
once obscure and blind yield warmth and light

how gentle and lovingly you wake in my heart
where in secret you dwell—fill me with love!

had she spoken or had she sung? she found his soul

speak to me, sing to me, grain of sand, never stop
tell me what you know, teach me, inspire me
reveal all to me that is precious to know on earth
make me your disciple, make me your shadow!

a shadow of a grain of sand? she teased
what good would that do? who could rest there?

from where is your knowledge? he asked

what i know is a memory, a faint light
a burning heart connects me to heaven
but gladly i teach you—let me search for more...

outside the dark night sank deeper and deeper
as the moon was veiled by the clouds of winter
but within there were apparent rays of light
there was a pre-established harmony of souls

she spoke to him, she sang to him

in the beginning was the Word, He lived in God
He knew in God infinite happiness

the Word was God who is the beginning
He was the beginning, He had no beginning

the Word is the Son born of the beginning
the glory of the Father is the glory of the Son

as Lover in the Beloved they live in each other
the Love that unites them is one with them

the Love is their equal, excellent as the One
splendid as the Other, making three in one

one Love among three, one Love in them all
one Lover, one Beloved, boundless Love unites them
for the three have one Love which is their essence

in that immense Love proceeding from the two
the Father spoke words of profound affection
and deep delight which were meant for the Son

my Son, only your company contents me
whatever pleases me, i love that thing in you
whoever resembles you most, satisfies me most
whoever is like you in nothing, will find nothing in me

i am pleased with you alone, o light of my light
o life of my life, o image of my substance

i reveal myself to her who loves you
i will love her with the same love i have for you
because she loves you whom i love so

my Son, i wish to give you a bride who will love you
because of you she will deserve to share our company
she will eat at our table the same bread we consume
she will know the Good and rejoice with us in Love

she was silent

from where are those words, grain of sand?
he asked after a long while

they are from God, she replied

how can you access them? he wondered

they are written in the library of love
they are composed for you and for many
they are spelled out in the book of eternity
they are your past, they are your future

where is that library? he wondered

within you, within me, within all people, she said

i wish to go there, he replied

follow your vocation and you will arrive
she answered, search within your soul
and the doors of the library will open
the words will flow like springs of water

contemplate and pray, become a great saint
honor God with your writing and your deeds
console God for the indifference He receives

can you show me more of the library of love?

o nightly visitor, are you truly unsatisfiable?
do you not wish to sleep in the small hours?

are you the night? he asked, how can i sleep
if the blessed night reveals her truth to me?

within the library she moved, sieving books
until she found the longing of tremendous love

alright here is a poem i have for you, she said

are you ready?

i am ready!

where are you hiding abandoning me in pain?
you fled like a hart after wounding me
i ran after you but you were gone

o shepherds, if you see Him i love
tell Him i languish, i suffer, i die

in search of love, i cross mountains
i fear no enemies, i gather no flowers
steadily i transcend all frontiers

o forests and groves planted by my Beloved
o verdant pastures has He passed here?

they reply: diffusing thousand graces He has passed
over those lands and clothed them in His beauty

she continues: who can heal me other than You?
send me no more prophets who do not satisfy me
they are recounting to me your unnumbered graces
but they wound me more and they leave me dying

how can i endure this exile not being where you are
when the arrows of love transport me near death
since you wounded my heart, why do you not heal it?
since you took it from me why do you leave me behind?

extinguish my misery because no one else can
my eyes long to see you since you are their light
i open them to you alone, reveal your essence!
let the vision of your beauty be my death
the longing of love is only cured by your presence

o crystal abyss, may your silvery surface
mirror forth the eyes outlined on my heart

He speaks: return to me, my dove! the wounded stag
is in sight on the hill, refreshed by your wings

she sings: my beloved is the mountains, the music
the wooded valleys, the islands, the roaring stream
the whisper of amorous breeze, the sounding solitude
the tranquility of the night, the approach of dawn
the supper which delights and deepens my love

our vineyard is flourishing, i make a bouquet of roses
may no one disturb us! cease deadening north wind!
awake loving south wind! breathe through our garden!
let your fragrance flow as we rest among flowers!

o fair nymphs of Judea dance under rose trees
but then do not venture to upset our peace
hide yourself, my Beloved, turn your face to the hills
yet have mercy on those traveling with me

His song: swift birds, leaping does, lions and fawns,
mountains, valleys, rivers, waters, winds and heat,
shadows of the night by lyres i adjure you,
let your fury cease, let my beloved sleep!

the bride has entered the garden of her longing
she is reclining her head in the arms of her lover
beneath the apple tree where your mother stumbled
i offer you my hand and restore you forever

her song: our bed is in flower, guarded by lions
built in peace, crowned by humility

there he gave himself to me and taught me his love
there i gave myself to him and promised to be his bride
my soul is taken, it is in His service, i guard no flock
i pursue no other goal, my only vocation is love

i am no longer seen on the common pasture
they say that i am lost and stricken by love
but i have lost myself and was found by Him

i weave those eternal garlands of flowers
with emeralds gathered on early mornings
each one is bound by a single hair of mine

with longing you observe my fluttering hair
you are captivated and wounded by my eyes
when you look at me your eyes imprint grace
you love me ardently and my eyes adore you

before i was unworthy but virtue and beauty
you have given to me before the world

He says: the white dove has returned
to the ark with an olive branch
she has found her mate on a riverbank
she lives in peace preparing her nest
guided by her beloved, wounded by love

she replies: let us rejoice now
let us go to the mountains where water flows
let us see the world clothed in your beauty
let us go to deep caverns concealed from view
enter them and taste the wine of pomegranate

there you will show me what my soul is seeking
there you will give me the breathing of air
the song of the nightingale, the tranquility of the night
the flame that consumes without causing any pain

no one dared to look at her, the siege was over
the hostilities ceased, the soldiers dismounted

when she awoke next morning she found the hut empty
she opened the door and saw him bent over a small fire
the smell of the food he was preparing made her hungry

she rejoiced in sight of him who was her spiritual brother
how much consolation was she to receive from his works!
the sun was gaining strength dispersing the lingering cold

when he saw her approaching he stopped his work
his eyes lowered he knelt by the fire and before her

good morning, my nightly visitor, she greeted him
little brother of my soul, confidant of my dreams

some dreams are to remain forever, he replied

which are those? she asked sitting down by the fire
and holding out her bare hands to warm them

would you care for some food? he asked her

are you offering your sister the onions of Egypt?
or the eternal word that springs from heaven?

i guess both are available, he replied

i am very hungry, she said

he poured water he had collected from a spring
he put a fish and asparagus on a wooden plate
still kneeling he offered the meal with both hands

i have no chocolate eclair, he said apologetically
she smiled, it would be too indulgent anyway

what are you eating, little brother? she asked
looking around to see if there was more food

my food is to do the will of our Father, he said

have you eaten already? she wondered

i can eat later, he replied

come now, do not kneel before me, sit by my side
let us share the meal which you have prepared

he hesitated, i have only this one plate

we will eat from it together, she replied

i have only one small fish, he argued

we will share it, she confirmed

remember, little brother, a shared meal is better
and more blessed than two separate ones

again he obeyed her

after they had finished eating he said to her
the village you are looking for is to the east
you will reach it from here in a day and a half

but where are you going? she asked

i came from the south and i am heading north
our paths crossed here for one blessed moment

she took a deep breath as sadness overcame her

our lives are devoted to God, he said, as you know

i do know, she replied

our commitment is absolute, he added

i am aware of that, she replied

in this realm there is only one encounter, he said

probably, she sighed

there are other realms, he said

of course, she replied

still it is hard, she added

it is, he agreed

he poured more water for her and she drank it
he cleaned the plate, then extinguished the fire

she got up, he stood before her looking into her eyes

then it is adieu, she said

here yes, he replied, but nevertheless, he added
only for one moment permit me to kneel again
before my eternal Queen and ask for her blessing

now she lowered her eyes

when i entered the hut yesterday evening
it was not fear that startled me but awe
your unexpected presence reached deep within
i recognized you in the instant of a moment

i am rarely known, she said, i rarely know myself

why is it like this? he asked

when i am not within i do not know myself
when i am within i do not exist separately

do you know yourself now? he wondered

i am in aridity, she said, in a tunnel of darkness
but i know who you are and i trust your opinion

he knelt down before her, this time she allowed it
may i ask in all humility for your blessing, he said

she held her hands over his head that was bowed
may the Lord bless you and keep you in His Love

refrain from seeking suffering for its own sake
but if you accept the suffering which is necessary
and cannot be avoided it will transform your life

my good friar in aspiration, remember not to worry
God watches over the affairs of those who love him

as the beloved becomes one with the lover
so God becomes one with all who love Him

if your work is destroyed by malady have no bitterness
powers are paying attention that are beyond comprehension
in one moment God can take the universe back to Himself

when you are imprisoned and separated from life
then pray for your jailers, they act out of ignorance
ask God to forgive those who trespass against you

kneel in your cell and offer yourself entirely to God
who gives you the grace to participate in his calvary
there are few who are worthy to be honored in this way

then remember the words and emerge from prison
with words of poetry of love and of devotion

souls transcend temporality like snowflakes
collect them in your love, your word is love
your vocation is love, your prayer is love

forgetfulness of created things
loving the beloved
remembrance of the creator
attention turned within

7.8

eventually the path reached the edge of the forest
and gave way to open fields and verdant pastures
she saw a small settlement with gentle hills beyond
in the air was saltiness rising from a nearby ocean

she noted children at play and milkmaids at work
she saw people tending the soil or herding animals
was this to be her abode for another breath of time?
was this where the story of a soul would continue?

all along the path through the tall woods
the nearly empty bag had grown heavier
while her abundant memories had dimmed
whenever she looked at her cold fragile hands
they appeared to become smaller and smaller

to enter the village she had to pass a gate
when she found no handle on the outside
she realized it could only be opened from within

she did not draw attention but resolved to wait
she reached into the pocket of her mantle
where she found a folded piece of paper

she opened it and slowly read the words
with this child i am sending you
an image of the goddess of wisdom

had the librarian slipped the note into her pocket?
but as she queried that memory it too faded away
librarian? what is a librarian? she wondered

she folded the paper and put it back into her mantle
she decided she would show it to the first person
who would approach—perhaps the mysterious note
was meaningful to them as it was not to her

she did not sit down but she simply stood by the door
she waited patiently, she was neither tired nor hungry
neither fearful nor confident but her heart was full of love

and now Beyond is dawning on the horizon, she said
but i thought Within follows Beyond, he remarked
it works both ways, she replied putting down her pen
a hypercycle! he exclaimed, a pair of written replicators

but i am longing to know the librarian's third answer
which was not provided, it was omitted, he insisted

naturally, she remarked

so far we have read that every book in the library
is about the Form of the Good and thus about Love
which were the first two answers but the librarian
promised to give three answers, do you remember?

i do, she replied

are you willing to insert the third answer? he asked
for those of us who have not guessed it by now

be patient! she replied, it will insert itself

❄ ❄ ❄

at this point the novice named John of St Matthias
—for reasons that are now known to us—looked up
and considered the issue they were discussing

if the third answer was not in the book until now
then where could it be? or when would it come?

was the librarian writing as she entered his office?
was the librarian in secret also an author of books?
was he the one who saw while others were blind?
perhaps he wrote down the answer on a separate
piece of paper that was elsewhere in the room

John looked among books and items on the desk
there was a wooden cross, a clay bowl, a japa mala
there were dried rose petals preserved for eternity

he saw the collected works of a poet and a saint
one of the books was open at the canticle of love
he looked up from the desk and saw on the shelf
the photograph of a young woman in religion

then he recalled that at the beginning of Beyond
there was this paper of a weightless kind
that had been spiraling between floor and ceiling
neither reaching one nor finding the other

was the third answer on the other side of that page?
he looked again and found what he was seeking
hovering in the air was the librarian's third answer!

he fetched the page and inserted it into the book
thinking of those who might benefit from seeing it
written down although it had been present within
from the beginning of time and before and beyond

it had been apparent between the lines of books
and not only there but on the leaves of the trees
the flowers in the garden, the swan's reflection
gliding over a still lake in silvery moonlight

❀ ❀ ❀

thank you! he said, this kindness refers to me
but i am astonished that we are now reading
about the novice who exists in a frame
that is beyond ours but not within ours

remember beyond is within, she explained
the grammar of creation is context sensitive
the logical parentheses are intertwined
all realms and all souls are connected

the librarian's third answer also began with a question
when God creates souls how do they differ? he asked

this is an intriguing issue, she admitted, because i am
confident God does not favor one soul over another
He upholds the symmetry in the all-redeeming love
which He pours out over the world and its creatures

yet it is our impression that souls differ accidentally
diversity is an undeniable fact, the librarian insisted

souls differ in their journeys through time, she agreed
they diverge in the trajectories associated with them

the difference demands an explanation, he pressed on
the individuality of souls asks for a subsistent cause
why do souls find themselves on varying trajectories?
how would you characterize the interaction occurring
between God and souls? the librarian probed further

for being God is the maker the souls are the creatures
for knowing God is the teacher the souls are the students
for purpose God is the lover the souls are the beloved

what is a student's pursuit? the librarian asked

learning, she answered

what kind of learning is required here? he wondered

one that encompasses all aspects of learning, she said

memorization? he asked

for sure, she replied

generalization? he asked

as in inductive inference? of course! she replied
it is needed to understand the world's regularities
the laws of nature and the meaning of life

and therefore . . . he paused

the soul needs a search space! she exclaimed

on his face was the smile she knew well by now

the library is the search space for the soul, she burst out
it provides the realm of possibilities sampled by choices
it is the initial condition which guides eternal becoming

God is the teacher of the soul, the illumination within
every school, every scenario of learning has a library
thus each book i open, each moment i live has meaning
offers an opportunity to grow, contains a message of love
is an attempt to find truth, points to the Form of the Good

if i wake up in the morning and find myself in a world
that makes sense i wonder: how does it come to pass?
the library is the answer! the library is the resource
for the soul to understand, to interpret, hope and love

and i kept asking myself: who assembled the library
who sieved books into an infinite subset of meaning?
and for what purpose? . . . she was exuberant now
she perceived all of the books as her devoted friends

let us make the library widely known, she continued
let us arise early and work hard to lead others within
for seeing the logos has the power to transform lives

you are right, my Lady, as a librarian i fully agree
let people come and find, let their lives be enriched
open the doors of the library, open them far and wide
feed those who are hungry, give them food of heaven!

in the moment of exhilarating silence which ensued
she contemplated her mission from a new perspective

yet there is another point i wish to add here, he said
permit me to repeat the question which i have posed:
how does God create souls that differ from each other?

she looked at him

then the full extent of the answer dawned on her
then she knew the answer, she saw it with a clarity
which suggested that she had always known it

she had known the answer
when awakening in the garden in spring
when floating in the warm pond
when sitting on top of the staircase
when walking through the museum
when conversing before the little cafe
when swimming in the ocean under stars
when running through the summer rain

with flowers in bloom and worlds being renewed
with willow trees dispersing the seeds of life
with the poem written in stone and on his eyes
with art celebrating the eternal female
with the revelation of love given and received
with bouncing photons from distant worlds
with each raindrop falling on her hair

those events and many others, perhaps all others
she now knew were God's gifts of love for her
she felt transported to another level of being

this library is not just any library, she said quietly
each soul has its own library assembled by God
but this library is my library!

the librarian looking within remained silent

while in her was again the moment of recognition
the breaking of bread at the supper in Emmaus
the *noli me tangere* at the morning of a new life
when this world and all worlds were redeemed

לא תגעי בי עדן לא עלית לאבי
Μή μου ἅπτου οὔπω γὰρ ἀναβέβηκα πρὸς τὸν Πατέρα
Noli me tangere nondum enim ascendi ad Patrem meum
Do not hold on to me for I have not ascended to the Father

this library is God's declaration of love to me
she said attempting to control her emotion

it is the specific logos offered to my soul
it is the point of departure for my journey
it is the continuous learning of my being
it is the encounter with the Eternal Word

the librarian nodded in affirmation

this library contains what God has prepared for me
to contemplate in the temporal and abiding realm
everything i find within is His affirmation of love

often i thought the books were my thoughts...
but in fact they are His thoughts...or ours...
His and mine...Heaven's and earth's...Eternity's...
the library is limitless, unbounded! *ewig, ewig...*

she fell silent

the librarian took up the theme of the conversation
(to bring the symphony to a conclusion)

this library is God's unending gift of love to you
the library induces your dreams, moves your thoughts
it awakens your mental images, drives your longings

the library accompanies your journey, your experience
your prayer, your devotion—it kindles your burning heart

the library is not only an arrangement of books
it is a garden of forms, an ocean of truth
a cathedral of infinity, an elated monastery
a mountain range, a firmament of stars

while each soul has her own library
and no two libraries are the same
all of them intersect in many books

if you encounter other souls in your library
they find you in theirs, harmony is established
journeys become linked, possibilities intertwined

the trajectories of all creatures form a bundle
for there is one God and one Creation
all libraries view the same limitless ocean
for there is one Truth and one Existence
but they are found under different firmaments
for there are many stars and many galaxies

there is resonance between libraries
as in causation between monads
many libraries share the same books
the same trees, the same waves
the same resting places of peace
there is pre-established harmony

but no two libraries are identical
the diversity of the creation
makes each library particular

each soul is uniquely loved by God
all souls are uniformly loved by God

all souls head to the same goal
they reach for the same blessing
they long for union with the One
but each soul goes on its own way

you are not alone in your library
instead you are called to interact
you are summoned into the world
but then the library stays with you

your exploration of the world
is a trajectory within the library
the library accompanies your journey
wherever you choose to go

whenever you find meaning in a sentence
the library is doing its work within you
whenever you see moment and eternity as one
you have an awareness of the library within

whenever you serve with a pure heart
you hold in your hands a beautiful book
you work in a quiet room of the library

whenever your soul wants to take
a little rest from the world's turmoil
you find an alcove in the library
or a bench in the garden of forms
a patio before the ocean of truth
a circle in the cathedral of books
an immovable spot under a tree
where you can be alone with God

in those quiet places you find the words
God has written for you or is writing for you
in the forever present because He loves you so

in those quiet places you find the words
you write for God because you love Him so

the library is your soul, your existence
the library is your being, your becoming
the library is the mathematics of those
the library is God's unending gift to you
the library is the story of your soul

the library is the structure of reality
it stands for a world with meaning
it enables a rational mind and soul
the library is the interaction between
the soul and the thoughts of God
it is the invitation to contemplate
forever the divine thoughts, the *nous*
it is the place where Love meets Truth

the library is both time and eternity
the library is the moment and the now
the unfolding of the past, the openness of the future
the eternity with God, His immanent presence
Her transcendent function, Their eternal harmony

the library is a school where we learn about forms
where equations appear, where ideas become mind

the library is the enchanted garden
where souls walk side by side
with the Form of the Good
or sit across Her on a table
and confer with Her face to face
in an unending revelation of love

the library enables you to see your own form
lovingly illuminated by the Form of the Good
which is the light outside the cave of shadows

the library is the place where free will emerges
the library sets the soul on fire and enables her
to do as she wills and even to will as she wills

the library is the reason why the world makes sense
the library is the reason why truth can be perceived
though the library is without time it is situated within
though the library is unchanging it responds to love

it is your fragile love that allows you
to participate in God's creation
it is your curious love that allows you
to read with astonishment
it is your creative love that allows you
to write with humility and inspiration

reading and writing are activities within
because all that is true is written timelessly

God is the author of all that is true
God loves you unconditionally
God is hungry for your love

the library is a projection of divine essence
unto the manifold of a created substance
the soul is the learner while God is the teacher

the library is the tool of divine illumination
the universal grammar of discrete infinity

the soul moves from one moment to the next
but each atom of comprehension is a book
some poems are longer others shorter
but each monad is connected to all others

temporality is the experience of moving
through particular books over certain pages
but God is simultaneously present in all libraries
for all souls are open books before Him

the limitless library which is called unending life
is the soul and all of its interactions in eternity
the library is the Logos, the Eternal Word of God
which resides in your soul and longs for union

as the Father loves the Son so God loves you
God became human so you can become Divine

EPILOGUE

drifting among scintillating stars in distant future
our descendants bring experiences of the Form
to places where she is both known and unknown

she is among them on meandering jumps in time
that lead to encounters with other origins of life

she is among them having solved the problem
of global cooperation on earth which is required
for stable coexistence of language-enabled life

her relentless love has brought them closer to God
tirelessly she weaved constancy and eudaemonia
into people's lives, hopes, longings, and dreams

she has moved them beyond confines of selfishness
her work has led them within where meaning emerges

it was not the fruit of a moment but persistent work
which extended over centuries and even millennia
it was the labor of virtue giving birth to peace

life—now based on love—is spreading in the universe
finding new places of wonder as the two realms fuse:
time is in flux, but what is is, what is not can never be

the nearby triple star illuminated the bridge of the craft
its light evoked in her a sensation of Saturday afternoon
in the small village near the ocean where she grew up

coffee from an earthly planet was steaming in her mug
placed next to some books which she had downloaded
from the extensive library of a passing molecular cloud
the joy of reading those books was in her future

ENDNOTES

Within uses italics to indicate quotes. Sources and inspirations are as follows:

Brian Davis, *The Thought of Thomas Aquinas*
Guy Gaucher, OCD, *Saint Thérèse of Lisieux—Story of a Life*
Guy Gaucher, OCD, *The Passion of Thérèse of Lisieux*
Gottfried Wilhelm Leibniz, *Discourse on Metaphysics and Other Essays*, translated by Daniel Garber and Roger Ariew
Keith J Egan, *John of the Cross, Poet and Mystic*
Plato, *The Republic*
Pope Paul VI, *Gaudium et spes*
Ralph McInerny, *St. Thomas Aquinas*
Sarah Coakley, *The Broken Body*
St. Augustine, *Confessions*
St. John of the Cross, *The Collected Works of St. John of the Cross*, translated by Kieran Kavanaugh, OCD and Otilio Rodriguez, OCD
St. Teresa of Avila, *The Interior Castle*, translated by the Benedictines of Stanbrook
St. Thérèse of Lisieux, *Her Last Conversations*, translated by John Clarke, OCD
St. Thérèse of Lisieux, *Letters* (Volume I and II), translated by John Clarke, OCD
St. Thérèse of Lisieux, *Story of a Soul*, translated by John Clarke, OCD
St. Thomas Aquinas, *Summa Theologiae*
William L. Rowe, William J. Wainwright, *Philosophy of Religion: Selected Readings*

❊ ❊ ❊

The Stanford Encyclopedia of Philosophy, edited by Edward N. Zalta and Uri Nodelman is a nearly limitless library. Countless articles have inspired *Within*. Some of them are:

Christian Tornau, "Augustine of Hippo"
Hugh J. McCann and Daniel M. Johnson, "Divine Providence"
Øystein Linnebo, "Platonism in the Philosophy of Mathematics"
Robert Pasnau, "Thomas Aquinas"
Ralph McInerny, "St. Thomas Aquinas"
Timothy O'Connor and Christopher Franklin, "Free Will"
William F. Vallicella, "Divine Simplicity"

※ ※ ※

3.6 is based on the Katha Upanishad

※ ※ ※

Within is entirely devoted to Thérèse of Lisieux, but Movement 6 in particular is based on the writings of the great Saint and Doctor of the Church. The sources are given below. The material is used with modifications to fit the structure of *Within*.

6.1 Thérèse knelt before her father before entering the monastery, 9 April 1888

6.2 Letter from Thérèse to Céline, 12 March 1889

6.3 From the diary of Céline describing their trip to Rome, November 1887

6.4 Thérèse carried this note on her heart when making her profession, 8 September 1890

6.5 End of manuscript A, presented to her sister Pauline on 20 January 1896

6.6 The Act of Oblation to Merciful Love, 9 June 1895

6.7 Manuscript B, Letter from Thérèse to her sister Marie, 13 September 1896

6.8 Thérèse's prayer borrows the words of Jesus, Manuscript C, July 1897

6.9 The ecstasy of St Thérèse, *My God, I love you*, 30 September 1897

※ ※ ※

7.6 Recites poems of St. John of the Cross, with modifications

※ ※ ※

Thérèse's last written text on earth was a prayer:

O Mary, if I were the Queen of Heaven and you were Thérèse,
I would like to be Thérèse so that you could be the Queen of Heaven!

                                                        8 September 1897

ABOUT THE AUTHOR

MARTIN NOWAK is Professor of Mathematics and Biology at Harvard University. He is a leading researcher in the areas of theoretical and evolutionary biology. He has proposed that cooperation is the third fundamental principle of evolution, alongside mutation and selection. His work has helped to create fields such as evolutionary dynamics, virus dynamics, mathematical oncology, and evolution of cooperation. He has published more than 500 papers and five books, including *Beyond*, which is also offered by Angelico Press. For many years, Martin has been working in the domain of Science and Religion. Before coming to Harvard in 2003, he held professorships at the University of Oxford and the Institute for Advanced Study in Princeton. In 2015 he received the honorary degree of Doctor of Humane Letters from the Dominican School of Philosophy & Theology at Berkeley. He is Roman Catholic.

Beyond the veil of confusion of selfishness lies another world, a world that is very different

402pp.
$21.95 ppr
$32.00 cloth

*B*EYOND IS A SOCRATIC LOVE story, a Platonic dialogue, a *Bhagavad Gita* of our times: a philosophical quest folded into an epic exploration of the world. Imagine an encounter with unconfused human existence. What does it mean to fall in love with God? Can the Good only adopt the role of a servant, or can it rise to provide a beacon of light ruling us? How often we are caught in the myopic perspective that the material world is all there is! And yet, mathematics and science themselves point to a greater, all-embracing, unchanging reality. This insight suffices to move past selfishness and advance humanity to the next level. *Beyond* dismantles the artificial borders that have for too long separated genres: here, science confronts philosophy, mathematics engages religion, poetry brings nonfiction to life, time meets infinity. *Beyond* is *sui generis*.

"What a marvelous and fruitful collision of the scientific, poetic, and contemplative temperaments, all in one author and one book."—DAVID BENTLEY HART

"*Beyond* moves from Plato to Augustine and Aquinas, to Krishna, Siddhartha, and the Tao."—DAVID HAIG

"The harvest of a lifetime of thinking about religion, science, and their explanations of the world, this book takes the reader on a Socratic journey of infinite discoveries."—WINRICH FREIWALD

"The truth is One, Martin Nowak shows us, and it is calling us to communion, even now in the concrete hospital ward of our lives."—JAMES MATTHEW WILSON

"Astonishment inhabits every line. I came away from it in a state of wonder."—MICHAEL MARTIN

www.ingramcontent.com/pod-product-compliance
Lightning Source LLC
Chambersburg PA
CBHW021140090426
42740CB00008B/859